PARADISE

GOD'S ETERNAL PLAN FOR
PEOPLE AND THE EARTH

JEFF MANN

Contents

Introduction

The Bible says that God "has planted eternity in the human heart" (Ecclesiastes 3:11). Think about that. When God created our spirits and knit us together in our mothers' wombs, He wired us to know instinctively that we will live forever. Why?

First, God wants us to know that we will never cease to exist. We are eternal beings made in the image of the eternal God. God built us to live forever, and nothing can ever change that. Death is not an end; it is a doorway through which we transition into eternal existence in heaven or hell. God has given us this life to choose where and how we will spend our eternal existence.

We are eternal! We are not temporary projects for God to play with and then discard. He made us with the dream of enjoying us forever. As a loving Father, God designed us to be His children and enjoy life with Him forever. Therefore, we were built to last!

Second, God wants us to seek Him. Why would God implant within us an instinctive awareness of our eternal nature? He intends that our instinct for true knowledge of the afterlife would cause us to seek Him. In response, the eternal Father reveals Himself to us, leading us into a glorious relationship with Him.

Third, God wants us to know the details about eternity. God doesn't intend for us to live in the dark concerning what eternity will be like. For this reason, He has implanted the awareness of eternity in the human heart and recorded the important details about eternity in the Bible for us to learn. God is the only one who really knows what eternity is like because He is the only one who has been there. Everybody else just makes their best guess, but God speaks from perfect knowledge. He wants us to know the basic facts about eternity so that we can make informed decisions in this life, not random guesses about how we should live.

When it comes to the subject of eternity, ignorance is not bliss. Some people prefer to ignore the warning in their heart about eternity because they are afraid of the truth. However, ignoring reality doesn't make it go away; it only leaves us unprepared for the inevitable. Ignoring eternity leaves us condemned to a life of foolish choices and an eternity of painful consequences.

Fourth, God wants us to know that there is a direct correlation between the choices we make in this life and how we will spend eternity. Knowing the truth about eternity is wonderful! It empowers us to live with insider knowledge about the long-term consequences of our present choices. Contemplating what the Bible says about life in heaven thrills the soul and emboldens us to persevere in right living with the joyful expectation of eternal rewards. Arming ourselves with understanding about the horror of hell motivates us to turn away from sin and sacrificially share the way to avoid hell with others. Those who stay mindful about the brevity of this life and the eternal significance of their everyday choices live each day with an enormous sense of destiny.

Moses prayed, "Teach us to realize the brevity of life, so that we may grow in wisdom" (Psalm 90:12). The purpose of this book is to empower you with biblical understanding of God's eternal plan for people and the earth so that you can live wisely in light of eternity.

1

Why Study the End Times?

The end times, or eschatology, as theologians call it, is the study of the return of Jesus, the events that lead up to His return and the events that will follow His return. There is a growing number of people in the world who are hungry for truth on this subject. They see the crazy things happening in society and instinctively know that something important is going on, but they don't know what it is or how to prepare for it. They have real questions. They are scared, confused, longing for substantive hope, and searching for answers. They are wondering, "Why are these things happening? Is there a powerful God who can protect me, give me peace and purpose, and help me make sense of this storm? If so, where is He? How can I get in touch with Him? Can anybody explain to me what is happening and give me hope? I've heard hints of prophecies in the Bible that talk about stuff like this. Is this stuff mentioned in the book of Revelation?"

This is a massive open door for evangelism! These questions are turning people's hearts toward eternity and ripening the harvest right before our eyes. We need to be equipped to give solid, biblical answers to their questions and point them toward following Jesus and living in His unshakable kingdom.

I experienced this firsthand when I met Say Tong, an Asian teenager from a Buddhist family, who knew very little about the Bible. He sat with me in a local park, along with two of his friends, asking me questions about the end times. One of his friends, Eh So, had briefly shared the gospel with him a few weeks before. By his own admission, Say Tong had listened politely, but was mostly disinterested in the subject until God visited him in a dream shortly afterward, awakening an earnest desire in him to learn more about Jesus.

Of all the questions he could have asked me to learn about God, Say Tong began with "What is the mark of the beast?" We opened the Bible to Revelation 13 and read what it says about the mark of the beast. I explained, "An evil, demonized man will arise in the future and demand that people worship him as God. He will insist that people willingly accept a mark on their bodies as a sign of their loyalty and devotion to him. He will demand that those who refuse to worship him and take his mark be killed, and nobody will be able to buy or sell anything without this mark. But God says that all who accept this mark of devotion to the Antichrist will be punished forever in the lake of fire for their idolatry. Do you understand?"

This, of course, led to more questions, and the conversation continued. I explained further. "There are two groups of people living in the world: those who know and follow Jesus, and those who are living in rebellion against Jesus, serving their own selfish desires. Jesus came to earth and died to make a way for us to leave the rebellion and be reunited with Him. It is now our choice to continue in our sin or to turn from our sin and submit to Jesus as our Lord. Soon Jesus will return to rule all nations on earth. Those who chose to follow Him will get to live forever with Him in His kingdom, but those who persist in their rebellion will be placed into a prison called hell for all eternity along with Satan, all the evil spirits, the Antichrist, the False Prophet, and all the other rebels. Does that make sense to you?"

"Yes."

"Do you believe this to be true?"

"Yes," he replied.

"Then which group of people do you want to be a part of?" I asked.

Both Say Tong and his friend Thatoo confessed, "I want to follow Jesus."

Two days later, Say Tong and Thatoo were baptized. I gave Say Tong his first Bible, and he received it like the treasure it is. We continue to meet for discipleship, and he is rapidly growing in his relationship with Jesus. He is diligently praying, reading God's Word, putting it into practice, and sharing it with others.

The gospel message proclaimed in the New Testament is the good news about Jesus' life, death, resurrection, return, and reign upon the earth.

Say Tong's testimony vividly illustrates how understanding the biblical narrative of the end times tells the story of Jesus. In fact, the gospel message is incomplete without understanding the return of Jesus, the final judgment, and His eternal reign upon the earth. Many believers do a wonderful job explaining the good news about Jesus' first coming, but the gospel message is incomplete without talking about His second coming. The gospel message proclaimed in the New Testament is the good news about Jesus' life, death, resurrection, return, and reign upon the earth. The subject of the end times is really the climactic ending to the good news about Jesus Christ. Interestingly, the biblical book that is most well-known for its end-times content is named *The Revelation of Jesus Christ* because the story of the end times reveals Jesus. Learning what the Bible says about the end times will equip us to answer questions, give hope, impart wisdom, and lead many people to Jesus in the great end-time harvest.

Many missions-minded enthusiasts get excited about reaping the final ingathering of souls to finish the Great Commission, but many are unaware of the context the Bible says this final harvest will happen in. Any good missionary knows that they need to study and understand the culture and environment of the people they desire to reach in order to more effectively communicate the gospel to them in their context. Well, the Bible tells us the context that the end-times harvest will be happening in so that we can effectively communicate the timeless gospel message in a way that is relevant to the world they will be living in. In fact, Revelation 14:6–11 describes a gospel message with a unique emphasis that is perfectly crafted for the masses of lost people living in the final three and a half years preceding the return of Jesus. The people of God who understand what is happening will powerfully proclaim this three-part gospel message with great effectiveness, leading to the salvation of many people from every people group on earth.

The growing appetite for truth about the end times is not limited to unbelievers. Many followers of Jesus are also sensing that something unique is happening in the earth right now, and they are beginning to search for information about this subject. This is a great opportunity for deeper discipleship that God is opening before us. I believe that God is purposely awakening a deep hunger among His people to understand the end-times scriptures because He is leading us into a deeper, living understanding of His eternal plans that will be strategic in bringing the bride of Christ into maturity.

Aren't the End Times Controversial?

There are many people who love Jesus, including myself, who have wrestled with feeling apprehensive about studying the end times. There are legitimate reasons that cause people to feel this way. End-times Bible passages can be confusing and weird when you first read them. If you combine the cryptic nature of many end-times prophecies in the Bible along with the sheer volume of how many of these passages exist, this subject can feel intimidating to begin studying. Some of these events seem so far out into the future that they can feel irrelevant to us. Many of the events the Bible says will happen at the end of the age are scary. And of course, many people who are really into the end times are either questionable in the way they interpret Scripture or divisive in the way they approach the subject and interact with others about it.

Many pastors are rightly concerned about the bad fruit they see coming from some who are fascinated by the subject of the end times, but who study and talk about it in a fearful and divisive spirit or get caught up in extra-biblical teachings and prophecies that do not edify. I have been in pastoral ministry for more than twenty years, and I have seen this many times. It is a real concern. However,

Why Study the End Times?

I don't believe the solution is to shy away from the subject, but rather to teach it correctly and model the right way to study and talk about it. This equips those we lead with wisdom to discern the false narrative and the wrong spirit so that they can avoid it.

I believe it is our responsibility as spiritual leaders to help people study the end times and interact with others about it in a healthy way. If we don't proactively teach people the biblical narrative of what is going on, they may get caught up in one of the many false, nonbiblical narratives that are out there. As a father and pastor, I don't want my children and spiritual children to be caught off guard by the unique challenges and opportunities they will face in the last days. I want to help them know the biblical narrative of the end times so that they are alert, equipped with strength and wisdom to stand firm in the Lord and shine brightly in the last days.

I have found that when people study the end times by focusing on learning what the Bible says about it and obeying the biblical exhortations of how to live in the end times, there is really good fruit that comes from it. The apostle Paul spoke of the positive effects that come from living focused on the return of Jesus, in Titus 2:11–14 (NIV84):

> For the grace of God that brings salvation has appeared to all men. It teaches us to say "No" to ungodliness and worldly passions, and to live self-controlled, upright and godly lives in this present age, while we wait for the

> blessed hope—the glorious appearing of our
> great God and Savior, Jesus Christ, who gave
> himself for us to redeem us from all wicked-
> ness and to purify for himself a people that
> are his very own, eager to do what is good.

When people live rightly focused on the blessed hope of Jesus' return, their love for God gets stronger. They grow in the fear of the Lord and become mature worshipers of God. They start living for eternal rewards rather than temporary pleasures. They pray more and have a growing appetite to study and obey God's Word. They see the eternal value of sacrificially loving their families, as well as their brothers and sisters in Christ. They give more attention to serving others, reaching the lost, and practicing spiritual gifts so that others can be built up in their faith.

Does God Want Us to Study the End Times?

In spite of the many challenges that come along with the subject of the end times, the Bible exhorts us to give earnest attention to these things, and even goes so far as to promise specific blessings to those who give themselves to understanding and obeying the end-time prophecies.[1] The end times is the climactic ending to the story God is writing. Who reads a gripping novel and doesn't want to see how the story ends? What happens to their favorite characters? What about the bad guys? Is it a happy ending? It is only fitting, then, that those of us who are

---

1. See Revelation 1:3.

so passionately devoted to God's eternal purpose should know how it will end. How does God finally get rid of all sin on earth? What is the fate of those who persist in rebellion against God? What happens to the faithful ones who sacrificially love Jesus and die in faith? Do they get rewarded? What exactly is their reward? Is it worth the sacrifices they are making?

God made great effort to record the details about how the story ends because He wants us to know in advance what He is doing so that we can be prepared for it. Listen to how the book of Revelation begins:

> This is a revelation from Jesus Christ, which God gave him *to show his servants the events that must soon take place*. He sent an angel to present this revelation to his servant John, who faithfully reported everything he saw. This is his report of the word of God and the testimony of Jesus Christ. *God blesses the one who reads the words of this prophecy* to the church, and *he blesses all who listen to its message and obey what it says*, for the time is near. (Revelation 1:1–3)

Did you see that? This biblical information concerning the end times is a message given to His beloved people from Jesus Christ. He went out of His way to send an angel to give it to John and have John meticulously record it exactly as he received it because He wants us to know about His return and the events surrounding it. If this information is that important to our beloved Bridegroom for His bride to receive, shouldn't we show our love for Him by giving our attention to it, learning it, and taking it seriously? Our study of the end times should be primarily driven by our heart of worship toward God. *Jesus, my beloved Bridegroom, if this is important to You for me to know, then it is important to me to learn and obey it. I want to know all about Your glorious return and the future You have planned for us together.*

When my wife and I were engaged to be married, one of our favorite things to do was to dream and make plans for our future together. We loved to talk about our future children and grandchildren, and the fun things we would do together as a family. We would dream about how in love we would remain as we grew old together, serving the Lord and winning souls. These conversations were strategic in bonding our hearts together and strengthening our devotion to each other. God was developing in us a bright hope and shared vision of His plans for us as a couple. Similarly, Jesus wants us to study what He has written in His Word about His future plans because He wants to have invigorating conversations with us about the kingdom that we will live in and rule with Him forever. These conversations will produce a shared vision of our eternal future with Him that bonds our hearts together with His in a deeper and deeper way. As we see our wonderful eternal future glimmering clearly before us, our fascination with worldly things will give way to a burning desire for Jesus to return so that the wedding can begin.

Jesus never says, "Don't worry about what the Bible says concerning the end times. You can't really understand it anyway." No! He says, "*Blessed* is the one who reads the words of this prophecy, and *blessed are those who hear it and take to heart* what is written in it." Let us decide today that we will be among the blessed. These end-times passages may be confusing to us initially, but if we will study them diligently and take them to heart, we will receive the blessing Jesus promised to those who do so. As we prayerfully search out these passages with a heart of worship, looking to the Holy Spirit for insight, we will gradually understand these things with ever-increasing clarity.

Knowing the certainty of our eternal hope in Jesus with such vivid detail enables us to see and delight in His beauty even more. His eternal plans and the process He will use to get us from here to there will cause us to marvel at His wisdom. The end-times Bible passages reveal many facets of God's nature, including the beauty of His love, righteousness, humility, zeal for justice, and majestic power. Gazing into these glorious attributes of God has a profound effect on our hearts. It produces a growing confidence in the excellence of His leadership, peace, steadfast faith, diligent obedience, and living hope that overflows in heartfelt worship.

Learning what the Bible says about the end times strengthens our hearts in a dynamic way, but it also enlightens our minds with wisdom. Knowledge of the future gives us power in the present. It enables us to make right choices today so we are positioned to benefit when those future events happen. For example, if I knew that a certain stock was about to dramatically increase in value three weeks from now, I could invest in that stock today so I would be positioned to prosper when it happens. If I knew that a terrorist was going to detonate a bomb at my local shopping mall in six days, I could make sure that I was not there when it happened. Better yet, I could alert the authorities and warn everyone I know so that many lives would be spared.

The Bible gives us 100 percent accurate and detailed information about what the conditions of the earth will be like in the years leading up to Jesus' return. It prophesies about the great revival that will happen at the end of the age and gives us instructions for how we can participate in it. It also tells us that all the nations on earth will go through a great shaking and describes the ways in which they will be shaken. Then it gives us specific wisdom for how to live so that we can thrive with Jesus, in our relationships, and in our ministries in the midst of those conditions. Don't you think that is worth investigating?

In God's loving-kindness as the shepherd of our souls, He has given us this information in the Bible so that we can prepare our hearts and minds for the challenges and

opportunities that are coming. Jesus even goes so far as
to tell us what will happen to those who are unprepared
when these events start happening:

> *People will be terrified at what they see com-
> ing upon the earth*, for the powers in the
> heavens will be shaken. Then everyone will
> see the Son of Man coming on a cloud with
> power and great glory. So when all these
> things begin to happen, stand and look up,
> for your salvation is near! (Luke 21:26–28)

Ignorance is not always bliss. Many people will see
the perplexing events leading up to the return of Jesus and
be overcome by fear because they won't understand what
is going on. Others who know the biblical narrative will
see those same events and be filled with a joyful anticipation of the impending return of Jesus that those signs
point to. God has given us all the information and wisdom
that we need to thrive in the midst of all the end-times
events that lead up to Jesus' return. His plan is not for us
to be among the terrified, but to be among the wise who
understand what the Lord is doing in that hour and therefore stand victoriously in Christ. The end-times drama
will break in unexpectedly for the ungodly, but the righteous who are familiar with the biblical narrative will not
be caught by surprise—they will be prepared. This is why,
after instructing the believers in Thessalonica about the
end times, Paul wrote, "But you aren't in the dark about
these things, dear brothers and sisters, and you won't be

surprised when the day of the Lord comes like a thief" (1 Thessalonians 5:4).

I don't want to be one of those who are overcome by deception, sin, bitterness, and fear in the last days. Therefore, I need to make time to study what the Bible says about these things and apply the instruction it gives. In this way, I am building my life upon the rock so that I have the strength to stand when the rains fall and the winds blow and everyone else is crumbling around me.

Jesus and the Saints Win!

When most people think about the end times, they automatically think about things such as the mark of the beast, the rise of the Antichrist, wars, cataclysmic natural disasters, and so forth. While the Bible does speak of these types of events that lead up to the return of Jesus, they are not the main focus. *The biblical focal point of all end-times prophecy is the return of Jesus and the establishing of His kingdom on earth.*

When studying the subject of the end times, it is essential that we study all these events with the same hope-filled perspective that the Bible has. When people fixate their attention on the difficult events that precede Jesus' return, they often become unbalanced and exhibit unhealthy characteristics such as fear, bitterness, and a self-focused, survivalist preoccupation. But when we read all biblical prophecies in light of the return and ultimate triumph of

Jesus over evil, we will abound in hope through the power of the Holy Spirit.

In a race, the focal point of the runner is on the finish line and the award ceremony that will follow—not the hurdles. He is aware of the hurdles that he needs to overcome to get to the finish line and prepares accordingly, but they are not his predominant focus. Similarly, the return of Jesus and His complete triumph over darkness must remain our focal point when studying the end times—not the great tribulation. The biblical end-times message is not about the domination of evil and the end of the world; it is about the total conquest of the kingdom of God over evil and the total restoration of the earth and humanity from the effects of sin and darkness.

The biblical focal point of all end-times prophecy is the return of Jesus and the establishing of His kingdom on earth.

The apostle Paul refers to this glorious appearing of our great God and Savior as "the blessed hope." This blessed hope is the fulfillment of what the saints have been longing for and creation has been groaning for throughout the generations. It is the ultimate transition point of history that liberates the earth from the tyranny of the kingdom of darkness so that it can flourish as God has always intended under the unified leadership of Jesus and His bride.

The End Times for Beginners

You can totally understand what the Bible teaches concerning the end times and eternity. The Holy Spirit is an excellent teacher, and He is excited about instructing us in these things and the good fruit that will come from it. The process takes time. Although there will be moments when you receive bursts of revelation and inspiration, understanding mostly happens in small increments over time.

For this reason, I encourage you not only to read this book, but to look up the scriptures that are referenced and read them for yourself in your own Bible to see for yourself if what I say is right. Then answer the study questions at the end of each chapter. Better yet, get together with a small group of friends to read this book and answer these questions together. We are all in the process of learning. Nobody has all the answers perfectly figured out, so be gracious and humble toward one another. Learn from each other. Lovingly challenge one another when someone shares a perspective that you can't see for yourself in the Bible. Don't be offended when somebody challenges your thoughts in the same way. This is how brothers learn together in a culture of honor holding God's Word as the highest authority. Remember, the Bible, not anyone's opinion or prophetic experience, is the only source for sound doctrine.[2] Doing these things will make this a much more edifying experience for you.

---

2. See 2 Timothy 3:16.

Why Study the End Times?

I am not someone who enjoys engaging in meaning-less debate over trivial subjects of theology. I study the Bible to know God and learn how to love Him better. I have no interest in wasting my time talking about sub-jects that don't practically help me to accomplish this life vision. I am investing hundreds of hours of my life to write this series of books because I am convinced it will help you serve the Lord and make disciples more effectively. I know that you are busy. There are countless things to do with your time, and now I am asking you to invest many hours of your life to not only read this series of books, but to prayerfully study the scriptures and become famil-iar with the basic storyline of the Bible. I know this is a big request, but I do it unashamedly because I know how profoundly it will impact your heart for Christ and those you influence.

With all this in mind, I invite you to join me on a jour-ney to discover what the Bible teaches about the eternal future of every human being as well as the earth itself. To understand what God has planned for our eternal future, we will start by examining the ultimate dream that was in God's heart for heaven, people, and the earth when He first created us.

Check It Out in the Bible for Yourself

1. Have you ever felt apprehensive about studying the end times? If so, what makes you feel that way? What are some of the mistakes people make when studying

the end times that get them off track? How can you avoid those mistakes?

2. What excites you about the subject of the end times?

3. Read Revelation 1:1–3. Do these verses encourage or discourage the study of Bible passages that speak of the end times?

4. Read Matthew 24. Does Jesus encourage or discourage people from studying Bible passages that speak of the end times? Pay particular attention to verses 15, 32–33, and 42–44.

5. What is the main thing that you learned in this chapter? How are you going to respond to what the Holy Spirit emphasized to you?

2

God's Eternal Dream

God is the greatest of all architects. A master architect is a master planner. Before the construction of a building begins, the architect has a clear blueprint drawn up detailing exactly what the building will look like when it is finished. Additionally, the architect also has a plan for the construction *process* detailing the order in which the building will be constructed. In the same way, God had a clear end goal in place for what He wanted His creation to be like and a detailed plan for how He would build it before the world ever began. The world is not spinning out of control, and God is not just reacting to current events, making things up as history unfolds. He is methodically and flawlessly executing His perfect plan for people and the earth toward a beautiful and happy eternal completion.

God's Eternal Dream

What is God's end goal? When all is said and done and His master plan is completed, what will it look like? Here it is: *God's dream is to live on earth with His people forever.*[3] Read that sentence again slowly and think about each part of it. If you can grasp that one statement, you are well on your way toward understanding God's plans for eternity.

God's dream is to live on earth with His people forever.

The first two chapters of the Bible (Genesis 1–2) describe the beginning of God's dream, where all the components of His eternal plan were installed during the creation process. In phase one of the building process, God created the heavens and the earth. Natural processes involving seasons, planting, and harvesting were established in His earthly creation. The heavens include the sun, moon, stars, and sky. The earth speaks not only of the planet, but also of everything else He created to live on the planet, such as trees, grass, rivers and streams, flowers, fruits and vegetables, land animals, birds that fly, and marine life. All these elements of life on earth were designed to continuously reproduce more of their own kind because God's intention was that all of them would continue forever.

But God didn't create the earth to live on by Himself; His eternal plan was to live here with people. So when He finished constructing the optimum earthly home for us to

---

3. One of my favorite Bible teachers is Asher (Keith) Intrater. His teaching has really helped me to understand the concepts I put forth in this chapter. I highly recommend his book *Israel, the Church, and the Last Days*.

live in, God proceeded to phase two of the building process and created human beings. People are the pinnacle of God's creation, made as eternal beings in His own image. Our eternal purpose is to live in relationship with Him, live together in families, govern the rest of His earthly creation, and to multiply and fill the earth.

Initially, God created two people, a male and a female. He placed them in a garden named Eden (which means "Paradise"), located in a geographic area somewhere in the Middle East, and commanded them to govern it. Then He blessed them to be fruitful and multiply. His end goal was that as the number of people on the earth increased, they would gradually move out and extend the boundaries of the garden until eventually the whole earth would be occupied by families of people living in close union with God, governing the rest of natural creation according to God's wisdom.

God's eternal plan for people was to live in an *earthly* home. He didn't make us to perpetually float on clouds in some ethereal, mystical state; He designed us to live in physical bodies in an earthly garden paradise forever. Our bodies were designed to enjoy clean air, aromatic scents, plentiful trees and vegetation, and an abundance of delicious fruit. We were made to live forever in an earthly environment filled with many species of multiplying animals, birds, marine life, and insects; life-giving rivers, springs, and bodies of water; and natural elements such as gold and precious gems.

The best part of God's plan revealed in the opening chapters of Genesis is that He was on the earth with people. He didn't just create people and leave them to themselves. He walked in the Garden of Eden with them, giving them wisdom and instruction to flourish in life as He conversed with them. God's cohabitation of earth with people was never meant to be a temporary situation. The Bible goes on to tell us that God's throne, located in the eternal city called the new Jerusalem, will one day be located on the earth.[4] When God created the earth, He was building it with the intention that He would live on this planet permanently. God and people will live here together, not just for a thousand years or even six thousand years, but for *all eternity*.

The Eternal Domain of the King

Throughout the Scriptures, God is repeatedly revealed as a king who is actively reigning over His kingdom. Since the word *kingdom* literally means the "king's domain," the kingdom of God refers to the *place* where His will is done and the *people* who submit to His leadership; it is the realm where God reigns. God's kingdom legally includes all that He has created; everything He made is designed to function under His leadership and according to His design.

For the sake of clarifying what the kingdom of God is and how it connects to God's ultimate dream of living

---

4. See Revelation 21:1–3.

on earth with His people forever, I'd like to highlight four aspects of God's domain. First, the kingdom of God is *spiritual*. His reign encompasses the spiritual dimension of His creation, which includes angelic beings, heaven, and hell. But the kingdom of God is also *natural*. His reign encompasses the natural dimension of His creation, which includes people and everything associated with human life on earth, such as families, governments, nations, education, business, architecture, science, technology, entertainment, athletics, and more. God's reign over the natural realm also encompasses the earth and everything associated with it, such as animals, agriculture, weather patterns, and much more. In addition to the earth, God's reign over the physical dimension of His creation includes everything else in the entire universe, such as the sun, moon, stars, planets, and all the vast galaxies that have yet to be explored.

The third aspect of the kingdom of God that I want to highlight is that His reign is *eternal*. The Bible reveals God to be an everlasting King who rules over both the spiritual and natural aspects of His creation eternally. Therefore, those who choose to enter the kingdom of God by submitting to Jesus as Lord will get to live in and enjoy the benefits of His leadership forever.

The fourth aspect of the kingdom of God that I want to emphasize is that it will ultimately become a vast *empire* on the earth, composed of many nations and people groups. An empire is where one king reigns over many nations.

31

For example, the historical Roman Empire had one king, Caesar. It had one capital, Rome, which was located in the country of Italy. However, Caesar's rule, laws, and culture were implemented throughout many nations, people groups, and lands beyond Italy that had been brought under Caesar's rule. Thus, it was not an isolated country, but a vast empire.

Similarly, the kingdom of God has one King, Jesus Christ. After Jesus returns, it will have one capital, Jerusalem, which will be located in Israel. However, the Bible makes it clear that ultimately the kingdom of God will fill the whole earth, encompassing every nation, tribe, and tongue. Throughout history, there has never been an empire that even came close to including the entire earth, but God's kingdom will. Jesus will be the King over all the kings and the Lord over all the lords. His rule will be enthusiastically implemented among every people group on earth, and the whole earth will be filled with His glory. Thus, in fulfillment of His original plan, God will live on earth with His people forever, and all the nations will delight in His wise and loving leadership.

Although God is the rightful King over all His creation, the majority of people living on earth and one-third of the angelic beings are presently entrenched in rebellion against His leadership. Consequently, God's will is not being implemented throughout the majority of the nations, and the whole earth is groaning in anguish because of it. The Bible makes it clear that this is a temporary problem that God is in the process of fixing even now. Jesus taught us to pray that His kingdom would come and His will would be done on earth as it is in heaven, because when all is said and done, God's master plan will be completed, and His righteous rule will be implemented throughout every nation on the planet, causing both people and nature to rejoice as the whole earth is filled with His glory.

The Big-Picture Storyline of the Bible[5]

The whole Bible tells *one* grand story. All sixty-six books of the Bible are put together to chronicle the one storyline of God's unfolding eternal plan for the earth and its people. We need to become familiar with this big-picture storyline of Scripture. The first three chapters and the last three chapters of the Bible act like bookends to the one grand storyline of Scripture. What God begins building in Genesis 1 and 2 is brought to completion in Revelation 21 and 22. In Genesis 1–2, God begins His plan. In Genesis 3, Satan sabotages God's plan. In the third chapter from the end of the Bible, God destroys Satan, and in the final two chapters of the Bible, He restores and finishes the grand plan He originally started in the beginning.

Think about the symmetry of the beginning and end of the biblical storyline. The first two chapters of the Bible and the final two chapters of the Bible show the following:

---

5. I learned the concepts mentioned in this section from a talk given by Asher Intrater titled *God's Plan Made Clear*. You can listen to it here: https://www.youtube.com/watch?v=ZUPIQnA6IyQ&t=1164s, accessed December 14, 2020.

Paradise

- God and people living together in blissful harmony

- God and people living together in an earthly garden paradise with the Tree of Life in it

- People ruling the earth in union with God

- The supernatural dimension of the heavenly realm of God's creation seamlessly intertwined with the natural process of the earthly realm of God's creation[6]

- People living on earth with no curse, no suffering, no sadness, no sickness, no pain, no poverty, no strife, and no death. There is only joy, prosperity, blessing, and abundant life.

God's master plan is described in its completed state in Revelation 21:1–6:

> Then I saw a new heaven and a new earth, for the old heaven and the old earth had disappeared. And the sea was also gone. And I saw the holy city, the new Jerusalem, coming down from God out of heaven like a bride beautifully dressed for her husband. I heard a loud shout from the throne, saying, "Look, *God's home is now among his people! He will live with them, and they will*

---

6. Presently, there is a veil separating the spiritual and earthly realms. There are angels and demons all around us, but we do not see them with our physical eyes because the spiritual realm is hidden from our natural senses in this age. However, after Jesus returns to earth, the veil will be removed and the two realms will be seamlessly intertwined under Jesus' leadership (see Ephesians 1:10). Imagine worshiping Jesus along with angelic choirs that we can physically see and hear!

be his people. God himself will be with them. He will wipe every tear from their eyes, and there will be no more death or sorrow or crying or pain. All these things are gone forever." And the one sitting on the throne said, "Look, I am making everything new!" And then he said to me, "Write this down, for what I tell you is trustworthy and true." And he also said, "It is finished! I am the Alpha and the Omega—the Beginning and the End."

I love verse 6 when God says, "It is finished!" The plan He started in Genesis 1 is finally brought to completion in Revelation 21. God then refers to Himself as "the Alpha and the Omega," meaning that the God who started the plan in Genesis 1 is the same God who finishes the plan in Revelation 21. The biblical storyline begins in Eden and ends in Eden. Thus, when everything is finished, God will live on the earth with His people forever.

> **The biblical storyline begins in Eden and ends in Eden. Thus, when everything is finished, God will live on the earth with His people forever.**

The storyline of the Bible has a beautiful beginning and a wonderful end, but what does it say about the cursed state of our world today? And what does it tell us about God's plan to transition the earth from its current state of brokenness and pain to the happy ending it prophesies will happen? We will answer these questions in the next chapter.

Check It Out in the Bible for Yourself

1. Read Genesis 1–2. What elements of life on earth did God build into His creation and intend to remain forever?

2. Read Proverbs 8:22–31 and Job 38:4–11. What insights do these passages give us into the creation process? What emotions did God feel about people and the earth as He created us?

3. Read Revelation 21:1–22:5. What aspects of life on earth do you see in this passage that are also mentioned in Genesis 1–2?

4. Read Ephesians 1:9–11. What does this passage tell us about God's master plan for heaven, earth, and people?

5. Read Micah 4:1–8. What does this passage teach us about the future of God's kingdom on earth?

6. Read Psalm 2. What does this passage teach about the kingdom of God?

7. Read Daniel 2:44. What does this verse teach about the kingdom of God?

8. For further study on this subject, go to my YouTube channel called *5 State Revival*. Look up the playlist

titled *The End Times for Beginners* and watch video 1, "God's Ultimate Plan for People and the Earth," and video 2, "What Is the Kingdom of God?"

3

Rise of the Rebellion

t is no secret to anyone that our world is presently filled with brokenness and abuse. In the United States alone, 1 of every 9 girls is sexually abused by an adult before the age of eighteen,[7] and nearly 1 in 5 women has been raped.[8] Globally, it is estimated that twenty to forty million people are being trafficked as slaves.[9] The scary part is that less than one-third of sexual assault cases are actually reported to the police.[10]

Poverty is another example of brokenness. One of every ten people in the world lives on less than two dollars a day. This extreme poverty takes a deadly toll, as 39 out of every 1,000 children die before the age

7. https://www.rainn.org/statistics/children-and-teens, accessed December 14, 2020.

8. https://www.nsvrc.org/statistics, accessed December 14, 2020.

9. https://www.dosomething.org/us/facts/11-facts-about-human-trafficking, accessed December 14, 2020.

10. https://www.rainn.org/statistics/children-and-teens, accessed December 14, 2020.

of five, and according to one report, 1 baby in 36 dies within the first month in poorer areas of the world.[11] I could go on with many more statistics of brokenness in our world today regarding things such as war, abortion, natural disasters, bullying, wars, corrupt and oppressive governments, religious persecution, murder rates, genocide, racism, disease, divorce, broken families, domestic abuse, theft, drunk driving, drug and alcohol addiction, and much more.

How did this happen? Brokenness and pain were never God's intention for people. When God first made the world, it was made according to His perfect design. There was no death, no depression, no poverty, no pain, no hatred, and no fear. The first two human beings, Adam and Eve, had a perfect, unbroken relationship with God (the source of all life), and therefore lived in a perfect, unbroken relationship with each other. Whatever they put their hand to would prosper. Wholeness was the norm as life-giving emotions like peace, love, hope, and joy dominated their inner world. Even the animals showed no animosity toward other animals or human beings. Everything was perfect and blessed. So how did this perfect world deteriorate to the point where today it is overrun with brokenness and pain? To find our answer, let's go back to Genesis.

---

11. https://lifewater.org/blog/9-world-poverty-statistics-to-know-today/, accessed December 14, 2020.

Sin Is the Pathway to Brokenness

As I stated in the previous chapter, God kicked off His master plan for people and the earth in Genesis 1 and 2. He placed Adam, the first human being, "in the Garden of Eden to tend and watch over it. But the LORD God warned him, 'You may freely eat the fruit of every tree in the garden—except the tree of the knowledge of good and evil. *If you eat its fruit, you are sure to die*'" (Genesis 2:15–16). God blessed Adam and his wife, Eve, to be fruitful and multiply while they cared for and cultivated the life within the borders of the garden. Their job was to enjoy God, each other, and the rest of God's creation. Over the course of time, the plan was for their descendants to continually increase and gradually extend the borders of the garden until the whole earth progressively became a garden paradise filled with God's glory and managed by people living in union with God.

God's plan was developing perfectly until Satan, an angelic being created by God, at some point succumbed to pride and the desire to be worshiped. He then enticed one-third of the angels to join him in a rebellion against God, which was swiftly defeated. After his attempted revolution in heaven was thwarted, he turned his attention to the earthly dimension of God's creation and sought to take it over by enticing Adam and Eve, God's delegated authorities on earth, to follow him in his rebellion against God. If Satan could get the leaders of earth to follow him, then he could control what happened on earth by manipulating people to do his will.

With stealthy guile, Satan took the form of a serpent and seduced Adam and Eve to disobey God by eating from the tree God commanded them not to eat from. Rather than resisting the devil's treasonous suggestion and using their God-given authority to crush the serpent, they foolishly yielded to temptation and became slaves of darkness. By disobeying God and submitting to a new, dark lord, the masters of the earth brought a curse upon everything under their influence—the entire earth.

The negative consequences of their disobedience were felt immediately. As soon as they ate the forbidden fruit, "their eyes were opened, and they suddenly felt shame" (Genesis 3:7). For the first time in their existence, they experienced negative emotions. Soon after that, they began to accuse and blame each other for their own sin, and it took only one generation for the first murder to occur. This tragedy is commonly referred to as "the fall of man" because God's ways of flourishing life and love were progressively replaced by darkness as selfishness, fear, and death became the new normal on earth. Under God's rule, the earth and its people had flourished, but now that the masters of earth had submitted to Satan, death and evil dominated. From that point on, sin continued to multiply in the earth, causing society to spiral downhill until today, where the whole earth is saturated with pain.

There is a moral of this story that we must learn: *sin is the pathway to brokenness and death—always*. There are never any exceptions to this universal law. To sin simply means to disobey God. Adam and Eve did not commit murder or engage in an adulterous affair in the garden; they simply disobeyed God by eating a piece of fruit that God had commanded them not to eat. To be sure, behavior such as murder, adultery, lying, hatred, and stealing are all sinful activities because they violate God's commands, but the root definition of sin is to disobey God. Similarly, when we disobey God, it will always lead us into brokenness, pain, and death if we do not turn away from it and embrace God's restoration plan.

Sin is the pathway to brokenness and death—always.

Thankfully, there is hope. The Bible reveals that God feels compassion for us and wants to deliver us from sin, restore us to Himself, and heal our brokenness. Rather than abandoning His plans for us, God set the plans into motion for Jesus, the eternal Son of God, to overcome both sin and Satan through His sacrificial death on the cross, thereby restoring man's broken relationship with God and recapturing man's authority from Satan to rule the planet. Thus, God's original plans for the earth, people, and His kingdom are back in motion!

Check It Out in the Bible for Yourself

1. Read Genesis 3. What were the negative consequences that came from Adam and Eve's disobedience?

2. Read Romans 5:12. How did Adam's sin affect the human race?

3. Read Romans 3:9–18 and 3:23. What does this tell us about the extent to which sin has infected the human race?

4. Read Romans 6:23. What does this verse tell us about the consequences of sin?

5. Read Romans 1:18–32. This passage is a summary of how sin has progressed in the human race. What stands out to you in this passage? How does God feel about sin?

4

The Take-Back Plan

G enesis 3 isn't all bad news. It also reveals that in spite of the sin and failure of mankind, God was still in complete control and had a plan to redeem both people and the earth from the curse of sin. Our brilliant God knew that people would rebel against His leadership and bring a curse upon natural creation. Before the fall ever happened, God had already prepared His plan to redeem people and the earth through Jesus Christ, which He immediately put into motion after Adam and Eve sinned.

The first step of God's restoration plan was to confront the rebels to explain the devastating consequences of their sin,[12] foreshadow the sacrificial death that would one day atone for their sin,[13] and prophesy Satan's ultimate defeat through another human being.[14] In Ephesians 1:4–7, the

---

12. See Genesis 3:14–19.

13. See Genesis 3:21.

14. See Genesis 3:15.

apostle Paul explained God's predetermined redemption plan in no uncertain terms:

> *Even before he made the world*, God loved us and chose us in Christ to be holy and without fault in his eyes. God *decided in advance* to adopt us into his own family by bringing us to himself through Jesus Christ. This is what he wanted to do, and it gave him great pleasure. So we praise God for the glorious grace he has poured out on us who belong to his dear Son. He is so rich in kindness and grace that he purchased our freedom with the blood of his Son and forgave our sins.

After the confrontation, God immediately banished Adam and Eve from the Garden of Eden to prevent them from eating from the Tree of Life, so that their sinful, fallen condition would not become permanent. If they had eaten from the Tree of Life in their sinful state, their fallen condition would have been irreversible. In Genesis 3:22–24 (AMP), we get to listen in to the conversation between the Godhead explaining their reasoning for this drastic move:

> And the LORD God said, "Behold, the man has become like one of Us (Father, Son, Holy Spirit), knowing [how to distinguish between] good and evil; and now, he might stretch out his hand, and take from the Tree of Life as well, and eat [its fruit], and live [in this fallen, sinful condition] forever"—therefore the

LORD God sent Adam away from the Garden of Eden, to till and cultivate the ground from which he was taken. So God drove the man out; and at the east of the Garden of Eden He [permanently] stationed the cherubim and the sword with the flashing blade which turned round and round [in every direction] to protect and guard the way (entrance, access) to the Tree of Life.

This was the moment when God separated the earthly and heavenly dimensions of His creation. Up until this point in history, they were seamlessly joined together, but God temporarily separated them until the full remnant of mankind would be redeemed, at which point Jesus will bring the two realms together again.[15] Everything in the heavenly realm still exists—the Garden of Eden, the Tree of Life, and the cherubim guarding the entrance to the garden with flashing blade. They are just invisible to those of us in the natural, earthly dimension.

God's intention was to first redeem mankind from their sinful nature before allowing them to eat from the Tree of Life once again. In Revelation 2:7 (NIV 84), Jesus announces this bit of good news: "To him who overcomes, I will give the right to eat from the Tree of Life, which is in the paradise of God." Once His redemption plan is completed, God will allow us to eat from the Tree of Life and live forever in our redeemed and righteous nature.

---

15. See Ephesians 1:10.

The Role of Messiah

After Genesis 3, the rest of the Bible tells the story of God's redemption plan unfolding throughout the generations as God progressively reveals Himself and His ways to the peoples of the earth through His covenant relationship with Israel. Through His dealings with Israel, God methodically set in place the scenario through which He would redeem the nations from the dominion of darkness and fulfill His plan to establish His kingdom throughout the earth. God promised to send a King called the Messiah (the Anointed One). This Messiah would be qualified and anointed to crush the kingdom of darkness and lead God's kingdom on earth.

Throughout the Old Testament, God gave us information about the Messiah so that we would be able to recognize Him when He came. In terms of His qualifications, the Messiah would be a human being because God had already decreed that human beings would govern the earth forever.[16] However, this would be the most unique human being ever because He would also be God.[17] The Bible prophesies that the Messiah would be a physical descendant of both Abraham and King David. He would be born in the city of Bethlehem, but His birth would be miraculous because His mother would be a virgin.[18] The Messiah would be a righteous man who was fully submit-

16. See Genesis 1:26.
17. See Isaiah 9:6.
18. See Isaiah 7:14.

ted to God. Rather than exalting Himself and misusing His authority for selfish gain, the reign of Messiah would be marked by righteousness, humility, and justice. In fact, the Messiah would willingly suffer and lay down His life for the sins of His people.[19] The Messiah would be anointed by the Holy Spirit for excellence in leadership by giving Him wisdom and understanding.[20] He would preach the good news to the poor and perform miraculous signs and wonders to liberate people from sin and the effects of sin such as sickness, demonic torment, and even death.[21] In the end, God promised that His Messiah would lead a redeemed, righteous remnant from fallen humanity to demolish the kingdom of darkness and establish God's life-giving rule in all the earth forever.[22]

In the course of time, the eternal Son of God became a human being and came to earth in fulfillment of the messianic requirements. Before His birth, God sent the message through an angel that His name would be called Jesus because He would save His people from their sins.[23] Jesus lived a sinless life in perfect submission to His Father in heaven.[24] He lived in perfect union with God, was anointed with the Holy Spirit, and "went around doing good and healing all who were oppressed by the devil" (Acts 10:38).

---

19. See Isaiah 53.
20. See Isaiah 11:2.
21. See Isaiah 61:1.
22. See Daniel 7:27.
23. See Matthew 1:21.
24. See Hebrews 4:15.

He gave us teachings to reveal what God is like and to show us how to rightly relate to God and one another. Finally, at the end of His life, although He was unjustly accused and innocent of any wrongdoing, He willingly submitted to a criminal's death on a cross to pay the penalty for the sins of the world. This was God's predetermined way to justly redeem fallen human beings for their rebellion, liberate them from their sinful nature, and restore the rest of natural creation from the curse.

Jesus accomplished far more through His sacrificial death than just atoning for our sins. He simultaneously redeemed *all* creation from the curse and met all God's messianic requirements to exercise leadership over the earth. On the third day after Jesus died, God raised Him to life. Then He ascended into heaven, where God the Father gave Him authority to rule the nations and carry out God's plans for the earth as a human King forever.

Today Jesus sits in the place of honor at the Father's right hand in heaven orchestrating His redemptive plans for earth, but He will not stay in heaven forever. In the fullness of time, He will return to earth to rule the nations as King in partnership with His bride—the remnant of redeemed humanity. Together, Jesus and His people will demolish the kingdom of darkness and bring an end to the curse over natural creation. The heavenly realm and natural realm will be joined together once again under Messiah's leadership, and the whole planet will flourish with abounding life as God and people dwell here together to fulfill His original dream for earth and humanity.

We Need to Enter God's Kingdom

The salvation that has now been made available to us through Jesus' death and resurrection is a vast treasure. He has made a way to cleanse us from sin and qualify us to live in the eternal kingdom that He is building on the earth. This salvation is much more than just forgiveness; it is an entire package of uncountable eternal blessings that we can receive for free. An official invitation to enter His kingdom has been issued to us. Our greatest priority must be to respond with wholehearted acceptance. The apostle Peter gave specific instructions for how to do this:

> Each of you must *repent* of your sins and *turn to God*, and *be baptized* in the name of Jesus Christ for the forgiveness of your sins. Then you will *receive the gift of the Holy Spirit*. (Acts 2:38)

To *repent* means to turn away from our disobedience. Repentance is first an attitude of heart where we commit to fully surrender to Jesus' leadership over our lives. We set our hearts to obey Him no matter what He asks us to do.

Turning to God is an essential aspect of genuine repentance. We cannot overcome sin and become a good person by our own efforts apart from God's power working within us. We must continually look to God for help, trusting in the Holy Spirit to work the miracle of transformation within us. We do this by diligently seeking God through prayer and reading the Bible regularly to discover God's wisdom and apply it in our lives. We also seek God by intentionally gathering with other believers to receive more of God's grace through our interactions with them. We don't just stop doing bad things in our own self-effort; we turn to God and receive His power to overcome sin and become more like Jesus in our character.

Water baptism is a prophetic act of obedience that we do in faith. It visibly demonstrates the miracle of transformation that is happening in our hearts when we are born again. The old nature and selfish way of life is dead and buried, and our new nature and way of living is being raised to life.

Receiving the Holy Spirit is also an essential component of our salvation. Without the Holy Spirit dwelling inside of us, we have no fellowship with God, nor do we have any power to live the godly life God requires. We don't need to be anxious about getting the Holy Spirit to fill us. We can't make it happen, nor do we need to convince God to do it for us. He is excited and eager to fill us with the Holy Spirit. All we need to do is obey what He commanded us to do. God promised that when we repent, turn to God, and get baptized, we would receive the gift of the Holy Spirit. We do our part in faith, and God will surely keep His end of the deal.

I distinctly remember an insightful question that somebody once asked me as I was explaining to them how to receive eternal life through Jesus. They asked, "If Christians have eternal life, why do they still die like everyone else?" I responded that human beings are made in three parts: spirit, soul, and body. Our spirit is where we commune and connect with God. This is where the Holy Spirit dwells when He comes to live inside of us. Our soul is our personality, made up of our emotions, thought life, identity, and self-will. Finally, we are physical beings with physical bodies containing our five senses of sight, hearing, touch, smell, and taste.

God told Adam and Eve they would surely die if they ate the forbidden fruit, but death didn't engulf all three aspects of their human makeup at once when they ate it. In fact, the Bible records that they lived hundreds of years after they sinned. Was God just exaggerating when He said they would surely die? No! Death instantly took hold of them when they disobeyed. First, they died spiritually as their intimate communion with God was broken. Second, death progressively worked its way through their soul and impacted their relationships as they became increasingly dominated by negative emotions such as shame, destructive attitudes such as pride, and defiling desires such as lust and covetousness.

Eventually, death climaxed in their bodies when they physically died.

Eternal life is restored to us in the same progressive order; it begins in our spirit, works its way through our soul, and climaxes in our physical body. Eternal life starts in our spirit instantly when we are born again. The Holy Spirit comes to live in our spirit, restoring our intimate communion with God. The Bible says that this indwelling of the Holy Spirit is a down payment guaranteeing the salvation of all three aspects of our being. The life of the Holy Spirit that springs forth in our spirit progressively works its way through our soul, bringing us into wholeness and affecting our relationships as we continue cooperating with the Holy Spirit in the sanctification process. Finally, eternal life climaxes in our body when Jesus returns and raises our physical body from the dead.

> **Eternal life is restored to us in the same progressive order; it begins in our spirit, works its way through our soul, and climaxes in our physical body.**

All Nations Must Be Invited

After entering the kingdom of God ourselves, our next priority is to share the good news about Jesus with others so they can have the opportunity to be liberated from sin and live in His eternal kingdom as well. Remember, the gospel of the kingdom is the good news about Jesus' life, death, resurrection, and return. Jesus said that "this gospel of the kingdom will be preached in the whole world as a testimony to all nations, and then the end will come" (Matthew 24:14 NIV).

This full gospel message will be proclaimed to all nations before Jesus returns. Why? Imagine a mighty king with an unbeatable army approaching a rebellious city in his kingdom to restore order, stop injustice, and reclaim what is rightfully his. In his mercy, he sends ambassadors ahead of him, offering terms for a peaceful resolution. If they are willing to renounce their rebellion, surrender to the king, and submit to his leadership, he will forgive their treason and allow them to live peacefully in his prosperous kingdom. However, if they do not accept his gracious offer, the king will arrive with his army, kill the rebels, take back his city by force, and restore order.

God loves every people group on earth and wants all of them to be included in His eternal kingdom. Therefore, He insists that before He returns to judge the wicked, rule the nations, and restore the earth, every people group must first hear about Him and have the opportunity to respond to His gracious invitation. For this reason, Jesus commands all His followers to "Go into all the world and preach the gospel to all creation.

Whoever believes and is baptized will be saved, but whoever does not believe will be condemned" (Mark 16:15-16 NIV). Every follower of Jesus is an ambassador representing King Jesus. We deliver His message to the nations of the earth, announcing the good news of His kingdom and inviting them to accept His offer of salvation by repenting of their sins and submitting to Jesus as Lord. Those of us who long for Jesus' return and the establishing of His kingdom on earth in fullness must diligently pray, give, and labor toward making disciples of Jesus among every people group on earth. This is the primary mission that Jesus commanded His church to complete before He returns.

Longing for the King's Return

Fellowshiping with the Spirit and finishing the Great Commission are wonderful objectives that we must do, but they are merely milestones to the ultimate completion of God's salvation plan. The return of Jesus and His reign upon the earth mark the ultimate finish line that the Bible points to for the completion of God's plan. Think about it: Jesus died to save us from our sins, but people all over the world are still slaves to sin. Jesus disarmed Satan on the cross, but demonic activity is still rampant throughout the earth. The Messiah is supposed to break the curse over the earth, but natural disasters such as floods, droughts, tsunamis, earthquakes, tornadoes, and wildfires still wreak havoc all over the planet. This is why the gospel message is incomplete and fails to live up to all its promises without proclaiming the return of Jesus to end the rebellion and restore all things.

The return of Jesus and His reign upon the earth mark the ultimate finish line that the Bible points to for the completion of God's plan.

Those of us who are born again rejoice in our new nature through the indwelling Holy Spirit, but we still long for our salvation to be completed when we receive our resurrected bodies and get to live on a new earth that is free from the corrupting influence of sin. In fact, the Bible says that the rest of natural creation is still yearning along with us for the entirety of our salvation to be manifested:

> For all creation is waiting eagerly for that future day when God will reveal who his children really are. Against its will, all creation was subjected to God's curse. But with eager hope, the creation looks forward to the day when it will join God's children in glorious freedom from death and decay. For we know that all creation has been groaning as in the pains of child-birth right up to the present time. And we believers also groan, even though we

have the Holy Spirit within us as a foretaste of future glory, for we long for our
bodies to be released from sin and suffering. We, too, wait with eager hope for the
day when God will give us our full rights
as his adopted children, including the
new bodies he has promised us. We were
given this hope when we were saved.
(Romans 8:19–24)

God's salvation plan has started and is progressing,
but it is not yet finished. His dream of living on a perfect
earth in a perfect relationship with His perfected people is
not yet fulfilled. How will God implement His restoration
plan on earth to literally end all demonic activity on the
planet, remove sin from the earth entirely, and break the
curse off creation so that bad things never happen again?
What process will God use to transition us from where
we are today, with the earth cursed and filled with rebellion, into the eternal kingdom of God, where the earth is
blessed and filled with righteousness? In the next chapter,
we are going to look with a broad scope at the transition
process the Bible describes for removing the kingdom
of darkness and establishing the kingdom of God on the
earth in fullness.

Check It Out in the Bible for Yourself

1. Read Isaiah 53; 9:6–7; 7:14; 11:2; 61:1–7; and Psalm
    2. What do these passages tell us about the Messiah?

Which parts of these prophecies has Jesus already fulfilled? Which aspects of these prophecies has Jesus not yet fulfilled (because He will fulfill them at His second coming)?

2. Read Romans 5:6–21. What specific things does it say Jesus' death and resurrection accomplished for us and made available to the human race?

3. Read Acts 2:38–39. What does Peter specifically tell us to do in response to the gospel message? What does he say God will do for us when we obey?

4. Read Romans 8:19–24 and 1 Corinthians 15. Why does it say we should still be longing for Jesus to return?

5. Read Matthew 28:18–20; Mark 16:15–20; Acts 1:4–8; Luke 24:44–49; Matthew 24:14; and 1 Corinthians 15:58. What does Jesus tell us that we should be doing until He returns?

6. What is the main thing that the Holy Spirit highlighted to you as you studied these scriptures? Write down specific ways in which you will obey what He has taught you.

5

The Two Ages of Earth

f I am casting out demons by the Spirit of God, then the Kingdom of God has arrived among you" (Matthew 12:28). Jesus made it clear in this statement that His kingdom is presently active and advancing in the world today by the activity of the Holy Spirit working through followers of Jesus. For this we rejoice. Yet the very fact that there is still demonic activity happening in the world shows us that God's kingdom is not yet being fully manifested in all the earth.

Living in the Tension Between Now and Not Yet

There is a great saying that says "the kingdom of God is *now* and *not yet*."[25] This quirky little sentence is really helpful to understand the transitional process God is using to remove the kingdom of darkness and fully establish His kingdom in all the earth. In Matthew 13:31–33 (NIV),

---

25. This concept was written about by George Eldon Ladd in his book *The Gospel of the Kingdom: Scriptural Studies in the Kingdom of God.*

Paradise

Jesus tells two parables illustrating that the kingdom of God is active in the earth right now.

> He told them another parable: "The kingdom of heaven is like a mustard seed, which a man took and planted in his field. Though it is the smallest of all seeds, yet when it grows, it is the largest of garden plants and becomes a tree, so that the birds come and perch in its branches." He told them still another parable: "The kingdom of heaven is like yeast that a woman took and mixed into about sixty pounds of flour until it worked all through the dough."

Today the rule of God is active in the earth like a little measure of yeast mixed into a large amount of dough. Although the visible expression of God's rule is minimal now, it is continually growing and will eventually fill the whole earth, providing great blessing to all God's creation. Although the kingdom of God is active and advancing in the earth now, it is also still coming; it is here in *part*, but not here in *fullness*. Many aspects of God's rule are to be experienced now, while other aspects of His reign will not be manifested until later. The Bible urges us to aggressively seek those aspects of the kingdom of God that we can experience now, even while we wait in faith for the kingdom of God to be fully consummated in the world after Jesus returns.

What can we experience now? Everything that Jesus did and experienced during His life can and should be experienced by us as His followers. We can enjoy internal blessings such as peace, love, hope, and freedom from sin through our fellowship with the indwelling Holy Spirit. We can also enjoy many of God's external blessings like His provision, protection, and deep, meaningful relationships. We can exercise authority over sin, sickness, and demons. We can even exercise God's authority over nature at times. We can hear God's voice, have angelic visitations, enjoy fruitful labor and ministry, and see God do miracles through us. We can see great revival happen as the Holy Spirit works in response to our prayers and disciple-making efforts. All these aspects of the kingdom of God can and should be experienced by us now. However, we will also experience persecution and the mourning that comes from living in the midst of a sinful and broken world, just like Jesus did when He walked the earth.

There are other aspects of the kingdom of God that the Bible says we will not experience until *after* Jesus returns. We will not receive our eternal, resurrected bodies until Jesus returns.[26] We will not experience the absence of trials and hardship, or the absence of sorrow and death until after Jesus returns. Worldwide righteousness and peace in every government and society on the earth will not take place until after Jesus returns. The elimination of sin, temptation, and all evil on earth will not happen until later. All these wonderful promises will certainly happen, but not until the time when Jesus has physically returned to the

26. See 1 Corinthians 15:23.

63

earth. We are to earnestly walk in the aspects of God's rule that are available to us now in this present age while also looking forward in faith to the fullness of God's kingdom that will manifest on earth when Jesus returns.

> **We are to earnestly walk in the aspects of God's rule that are available to us now in this present age while also looking forward in faith to the fullness of God's kingdom that will manifest on earth when Jesus returns.**

Hannah is a beautiful picture of God's kingdom advancing in the world today. My wife and I met Hannah many years ago when she was a broken teenage girl longing for freedom from sin and healing from the effects of sin. When we first met her, she was addicted to drugs, living in disobedience to God, and tormented by evil spirits, but she knew the gospel and believed that Jesus could deliver her from Satan's power. She transferred from the kingdom of darkness to the kingdom of God when she repented of her sin and made Jesus Lord of her life. The Holy Spirit met her in a powerful way and progressively healed her soul. As she continued yielding to Jesus' leadership, He delivered her from the demonic affliction and set her free from drug addiction. Today she is a dynamic wife, mother, and a powerful woman of God. She is full of the Holy Spirit with a strong prophetic and evangelistic gift. She sacrificially pours her life into loving the lost and ministering Christ's salvation to many who are bound by sin, alcoholism, drug addiction, and demonic spirits.

Hannah was once a slave in the kingdom of darkness, but now is a free daughter of God living under God's rule in this present age. However, Hannah still faces struggles. Sometimes she gets sick and suffers from allergies. She frequently feels tired because of a lack of sleep that stems from being the mother of four beautiful little girls who don't yet always sleep through the night. Occasionally, she endures persecution and mistreatment because of her choice to live a godly life and boldly proclaim Jesus to others. Like everyone else who shines brightly for Jesus in this age, Hannah has to deal with spiritual warfare, fighting through demonic attacks as the enemy tries to discourage and harass her. She rejoices when those she loves experience God and grow closer to Jesus, but she also mourns when those she is investing in choose to sin, bringing harm to themselves and others.

Although Hannah is experiencing many of the benefits of living in the kingdom of God right now, she is also very aware that she is not presently experiencing *all* the benefits promised to her in the Bible. She is not living in her eternal, resurrected body yet or in a world that is without sin and brokenness. This is because we are presently living in a unique season of history on earth where both the kingdom of God and the kingdom of darkness are active.

The Two Ages of Earth

The Bible speaks of two time periods on earth, known as *this present evil age* and *the age to come*. During this present evil age, the majority of the people living on earth are significantly being influenced by evil spirits and sinful desires. Therefore, the culture on earth during this present age is largely dominated by evil, wickedness, and rebellion against the will of God. We can see this clearly in Ephesians 2:2–3:

> You used to live in sin, just like the rest of the world, *obeying the devil—the commander of the powers in the unseen world. He is the spirit at work in the hearts of those who refuse to obey God.* All of us used to live that way, *following the passionate desires and inclinations of our sinful nature.* By our very nature we were subject to God's anger, just like everyone else.

Whereas this present age is characterized by sin and the curse, the age to come will be marked by righteousness, peace, joy, prosperity, and the abundant blessings that accompany Jesus' reign. This is because all demonic activity will be removed from the earth, and God's rule will be the predominant influence in the age to come. This present age is the season where the kingdom of darkness is rampant in the earth; the age to come is the eternal age of God's kingdom being fully expressed throughout every aspect of life on earth.

The Two Ages of Earth

This present evil age on earth has a beginning and an end; it began with the fall of man in Genesis 3 and ends when Jesus returns. The age to come also has a beginning, but it has no end; it begins with the second coming of Jesus but continues forever. In light of eternity, this present evil age will end up being a very short season of the earth's history. Sin, brokenness, and death seem normal to us now because it has been this way for thousands of years. However, billions of years from now, we will look back on this short six-thousand-year season and say, "Remember when most people thought it was a good idea to disobey God, and there were things like poverty and hatred and immorality and death and fear that permeated society? That was so long ago. What a crazy season that was! I'm so glad that is over, and now we get to live here with Jesus far removed from all that dark stuff!"

There is an overlap between the two ages. The breaking in of God's kingdom was inaugurated with Jesus' first coming and will be consummated with Jesus' second coming. Followers of Jesus have the kingdom of God growing within them now as the Holy Spirit progressively helps them submit to Jesus' leadership in the many facets of their lives. Even now the kingdom of God is progressively growing in the earth as more and more people hear the gospel and submit to Jesus as Lord.

The Bible calls us believers because we believe the biblical message about the kingdom of God coming and the age of sin coming to an end. Therefore, we respond by turning from our rebellion and submitting to Jesus as Lord in this present age in order to be on the winning team when the age to come arrives. This is exactly why Jesus exhorted everyone to "repent of your sins and turn to God, for the Kingdom of Heaven is near" (Matthew 4:17). The fact that we are presently able to experience certain aspects of the kingdom of God in this age is a foretaste to confirm our faith that the fullness of God's kingdom will be experienced in the age to come. For sure, there is a real measure of sacrifice involved when we live for Jesus in the midst of a sinful culture that hates God's rule, but Jesus encourages us that such sacrifices in this present age will be rewarded richly in the age to come.

> "I tell you the truth," Jesus replied, "no one who has left home or brothers or sisters or mother or father or children or fields for me and the gospel will fail to receive a hundred times as much in *this present age* (homes, brothers, sisters, mothers, children and fields—and with them, persecutions) and in the *age to come*, eternal life. But many who are first will be last, and the last first." (Mark 10:29–31 NIV84)

The Great Harvest of Earth

What can we expect life to be like as we approach the end of this present age? Darkness will get even darker while light continues growing brighter. In Matthew 13:24–30

The Two Ages of Earth

(NIV), Jesus told a parable illustrating how sin and righteousness will both grow to maturity until the end of this present evil age, when there will be a *great harvest* of judgment for the wicked and blessing for the righteous. I see this parable as Jesus' summary of world history from God's perspective:

> Jesus told them another parable: "The kingdom of heaven is like a man [Jesus] who sowed good seed [righteous people] in his field [the earth]. But while everyone was sleeping, his enemy [Satan] came and sowed weeds [evil people] among the wheat, and went away. When the wheat sprouted and formed heads, then the weeds also appeared.
>
> "The owner's servants came to him and said, 'Sir, didn't you sow good seed in your field? Where then did the weeds come from?'
>
> "'An enemy did this,' he replied. The servants asked him, 'Do you want us to go and pull them up?'
>
> "'No,' he answered, 'because while you are pulling the weeds, you may uproot the wheat with them. Let both grow together until the harvest [the end of the age]. At that time I will tell the harvesters [angels]: First collect the weeds and tie them in bundles to be burned [hell]; then gather the wheat and bring it into my barn [the kingdom of God].'"

Paradise

Shortly after sharing the parable, Jesus explained it to us in Matthew 13:36–43 (NIV):

> His disciples came to him and said, "Explain to us the parable of the weeds in the field."
>
> He answered, "The one who sowed the good seed is the Son of Man. The field is the world, and the good seed stands for the people of the kingdom. The weeds are the people of the evil one, and the enemy who sows them is the devil. The harvest is the end of the age, and the harvesters are angels.
>
> "As the weeds are pulled up and burned in the fire, so it will be at the end of the age. The Son of Man will send out his angels, and they will weed out of his kingdom everything that causes sin and all who do evil. They will throw them into the blazing furnace, where there will be weeping and gnashing of teeth. Then the righteous will shine like the sun in the kingdom of their Father. He who has ears, let them hear."

People often mistakenly refer to the end times as the end of the world. It's not the end of the world; it is the end of this present evil age on earth and the dawning of the new and glorious age of the eternal kingdom of God. As we transition from this evil age to the age to come, both the rebellion and the righteous remnant will ripen unto maturity and fully blossom. Then the two crops of earth will be harvested at the end of the age. All the rebels will be removed from earth and condemned to eternal punishment in a prison called the lake of fire. The righteous remnant will be rewarded with eternal living in God's kingdom on a sinless earth. The earth will not die; it will simply transition from being primarily led by demons and sinful people to being governed by God and the saints. Therefore, the term *last days* does not refer to the last days of the earth, but the last days of this present evil age, for which we rejoice!

We Have a Choice to Make

The story of Jesus, His kingdom, and the rebellion on earth has many parallels to the classic tale of *Robin Hood*. In that story, the true king of England is a good man named Richard. He is away from the country for a period of time and appoints Prince John to rule in his place until he returns. Rather than serving the people as King Richard would, Prince John misuses his authority for selfish gain, oppressing the people and declaring open rebellion against King Richard. Those who remain loyal to King Richard are persecuted for their loyalty. When the rightful king returns, he takes his designated place of leadership, gets rid of the evil ones who resisted his rule, and rewards those who were loyal to him by publicly honoring them and promoting them to positions of leadership in his kingdom. The rebellion is crushed, and a time of prosperity and joy comes to the land as King Richard rules justly in partnership with his loyal people.

Because God is good and holy, He will permanently fix the problem of evil in the world.

Because God is good and holy, He will permanently fix the problem of evil in the world. Plan A is *mercy*. If we will repent, God will forgive us and transform us. This will fix the problem of evil in us through what Jesus did on the cross and our willing cooperation with the Holy Spirit as He sanctifies us. Plan B for getting rid of evil in the world is *God's wrath and judgment*. For those who reject God's mercy, God will still fix the problem of evil by imprisoning them in hell forever. Plan A is God's preferred method for fixing the problem of evil, but we get to choose which method God uses with us. We can humble ourselves, repent, and cooperate with God's mercy to get rid of our sin, or we can stubbornly harden our hearts to persist in our rebellion and experience God's wrath. Either way, God will manifest His goodness by fixing the problem of evil in the world without violating our free will.

We have seen that as we transition into the coming age of Jesus' reign, there will be a final judgment where Jesus separates the wicked from the righteous. The righteous will live blissfully with Him in His kingdom on earth forever, while the wicked will be imprisoned forever in the lake of fire. In the next chapter, we will examine what the Bible says about the final state of the rebels.

Check It Out in the Bible for Yourself

1. Read 1 Corinthians 15:1–28. What aspects of God's reign can we experience now in this present age? What aspects of God's reign will we not experience until after Jesus returns?

2. Read Matthew 13:47–50 and 2 Thessalonians 1:3–10. Why is it necessary for Jesus to judge and punish the wicked when He returns?

3. What new things have you learned from reading this chapter and studying these passages? What questions do you still have? What will you do to apply what you have learned and find biblical answers to the questions you still have?

4. For further study, go to my YouTube channel called *5 State Revival*. Look up the playlist titled *The End Times for Beginners* and watch video 3, "The Kingdom of God is NOW and NOT YET," and video 4, "The Two Ages of Earth."

6

Lake of Fire: The Final End of the Rebellion

The good news about Jesus' first coming is that we can be forgiven of sin and restored to a right relationship with God because of His life, death, and resurrection. But the good news about Jesus doesn't stop there. Although sin continues to run rampant throughout the earth today, Jesus will return to ensure that the rebellion on earth comes to a complete and permanent end. The good news about Jesus' second coming is that all sin and its corresponding negative consequences will be removed from the planet forever so that only righteousness, justice, and blessing will remain. Those who choose to repent of their sin and follow Jesus will get to live in Garden of Eden–like conditions on a perfect and sinless earth, enjoying the pleasures of His kingdom forever.

But what about those who choose not to repent and submit to Jesus as their Lord? What does the Bible tell us about the eternal state of the rebels? Scripture makes it clear that every single person will face a final judgment where they will give an account to God for their life choices. The righteous will be rewarded with eternal life in the kingdom of God, while the wicked will suffer eternal punishment in a prison called the lake of fire. In Romans 2:5–10, the apostle Paul spoke of this final judgment:

> For a day of anger is coming, when God's righteous judgment will be revealed. *He will judge everyone according to what they have done.* He will give eternal life to those who keep on doing good, seeking after the glory and honor and immortality that God offers. But he will pour out his anger and wrath on those who live for themselves, who refuse to obey the truth and instead live lives of wickedness. There will be trouble and calamity for everyone who keeps on doing what is evil—for the Jew first and also for the Gentile. But there will be glory and honor and peace from God for all who do good—for the Jew first and also for the Gentile.

The apostle John describes this final judgment in Revelation 20:12–15:

> I saw the dead, both great and small, standing before God's throne. And the books were opened, including the Book of Life.

> And the dead were judged according to what they had done, as recorded in the books. The sea gave up its dead, and death and the grave gave up their dead. *And all were judged according to their deeds.* Then death and the grave were thrown into the lake of fire. This lake of fire is the second death. *And anyone whose name was not found recorded in the Book of Life was thrown into the lake of fire.*

Those who respond to the good news about Jesus' death and resurrection by renouncing their sinful ways and following Jesus as Lord have their names recorded in the Book of Life. Those whose names are not found written in the Book of Life will be banished to the lake of fire. This is confirmed by God Himself just a few verses later in Revelation 21:7–8. After announcing the glorious coming of the new heavens and new earth and the complete removal of the curse, God proclaims that all who are victorious over sin through Jesus "will inherit all these blessings, and I will be their God, and they will be my children. But cowards, unbelievers, the corrupt, murderers, the immoral, those who practice witchcraft, idol worshipers, and all liars—*their fate is in the fiery lake of burning sulfur.* This is the second death."

The impending promises of final deliverance from persecution for the righteous and the corresponding eternal punishment of the wicked are spoken of again by the apostle Paul in his letter to the believers in Thessalonica:

> And God will provide rest for you who are being persecuted and also for us when the Lord Jesus appears from heaven. He will come with his mighty angels, in flaming fire, bringing judgment on those who don't know God and on those who refuse to obey the Good News of our Lord Jesus. *They will be punished with eternal destruction, forever separated from the Lord and from his glorious power.* When he comes on that day, he will receive glory from his holy people—praise from all who believe. And this includes you, for you believed what we told you about him. (2 Thessalonians 1:7–10)

The two options for life in the age to come are summed up by Jesus in Matthew 25:46, where He says that the wicked "will go away into eternal punishment, but the righteous will go into eternal life." What, specifically, does the Bible say about this eternal punishment? What will hell really be like for the wicked?

People Were Not Created to Live in Hell

It was never God's intent for people to live in hell forever. Jesus made this interesting statement in Matthew 25:41 (NIV) when condemning the wicked to the lake of fire:

Depart from me, you who are cursed, into the eternal fire *prepared for the devil and his angels*.

Hell was created for the rebels, but people were not created for rebellion. However, when people willingly choose to join the demonic host in rebelling against God, they subject themselves to the same punishment.

Hell was created as the place of punishment for those who refused to submit to God. It was made as an eternal prison for Satan and the angels who joined him in his rebellion against God. Hell was created for the rebels, but people were not created for rebellion. People were created to live forever in blissful union with God and each other under Jesus' loving leadership. However, when people willingly choose to join the demonic host in rebelling against God, they subject themselves to the same punishment. Because God is a righteous judge who shows no partiality, all who rebel against Him go to the same prison. Later, Jesus made this interesting statement regarding the ministry of the Holy Spirit:

> And when he comes, he will convict the
> world of its sin, and of God's righteousness,
> and of the coming judgment. The world's sin
> is that it refuses to believe in me. Righteous-
> ness is available because I go to the Father,
> and you will see me no more. *Judgment will
> come because the ruler of this world has
> already been judged.* (John 16:8–11)

The Holy Spirit convinces us with power of our guilt
in regard to sin. He also convinces us of the availability of
the gift of righteousness through faith in Jesus if we will
repent. Finally, He convinces us of the solemn certainty
of coming judgment for our rebellion if we do not repent.
How do we know this? Because Satan, the original rebel,
has already been sentenced to eternal punishment in hell;
therefore, the rest of the rebels are assured of the same
fate unless they escape the rebellion through the avenue
God has provided (following Jesus).

Hell Is a Place of Physical Torment

As we have already seen in many of the Bible passages above, the final place of punishment for those who
persist in rebellion against God is vividly described as
a lake of fire. When I try to imagine what a lake of fire
could be, I think of the molten lava that flows out of an
erupting volcano.

Imagine how awful it would be to have every part of
your body immersed in lava without even a moment of

reprieve for all eternity. I think of times when I've made the mistake of touching something scalding hot for just a fraction of a second and burned my finger. I immediately pulled my hand away and soaked my finger in cold water, yet the pain of the burn continued to sting for hours—and that was just a little burn that lasted less than a second. Imagine the agony of burning that never stops.

It is horrifying to think of suffering this intense, yet this is how Jesus describes the experience of those who are sentenced to hell. Consider the following statement Jesus made in Mark 9:47–48 (GNT):

> And if your eye makes you lose your faith, take it out! It is better for you to enter the Kingdom of God with only one eye than to keep both eyes and be thrown into hell. *There 'the worms that eat them never die, and the fire that burns them is never put out.'*

Here Jesus describes yet another element of suffering in hell when He says that "the worms that eat them never die." Normally, when a dead body is left to rot, worms feed on it until there is nothing left to eat. However, the worms in hell are able to feed on flesh and never die, apparently because they always have flesh to feed on. Similarly, Jesus said that "the fire that burns them is never put out." Fire must have fuel to continue burning. It seems that despite the burning of skin and worms eating on flesh, the bodies in this lake of fire somehow continue to remain and the physical suffering never stops. Are you beginning to understand why it is such good news that Jesus took our punishment on the cross so we could avoid this place?

This is not the only time that Jesus warned about the physical torment experienced in hell. In another setting Jesus told the following story:

> Jesus said, "There was a certain rich man who was splendidly clothed in purple and fine linen and who lived each day in luxury. At his gate lay a poor man named Lazarus who was covered with sores. As Lazarus lay there longing for scraps from the rich man's table, the dogs would come and lick his open sores.
>
> "Finally, the poor man died and was carried by the angels to be with Abraham. The rich man also died and was buried, and his soul went to the place of the dead. There, in torment, he saw Abraham in the far distance with Lazarus at his side.
>
> "The rich man shouted, 'Father Abraham, have some pity! Send Lazarus over here to dip the tip of his finger in water and cool my tongue. I am in anguish in these flames.'
>
> "But Abraham said to him, 'Son, remember that during your lifetime you had everything you wanted, and Lazarus had nothing. So now he is here being comforted, and you are in anguish. And besides, there is a great chasm separating us. No one can cross over

to you from here, and no one can cross over to us from there.'

"Then the rich man said, 'Please, Father Abraham, at least send him to my father's home. For I have five brothers, and I want him to warn them so they don't end up in this place of torment.'

"But Abraham said, 'Moses and the prophets have warned them. Your brothers can read what they wrote.'

"The rich man replied, 'No, Father Abraham! But if someone is sent to them from the dead, then they will repent of their sins and turn to God.'

"But Abraham said, 'If they won't listen to Moses and the prophets, they won't be persuaded even if someone rises from the dead.'" (Luke 16:19–31)

What can we learn from Jesus' description of hell in this story? First, hell is a place of extreme bodily suffering. Twice in this story, hell is described as a place of torment. In fact, the rich man in Jesus' story exclaimed, "I am in anguish in these flames." His suffering was not just spiritual, but physical. He was not a disembodied soul that was suffering in some mystical way. We know that he had a physical body because he wanted water to place on his tongue and had the ability to speak and even shout.

Hell Is a Place of Emotional Torment

Another lesson we can learn about hell from the story of the rich man and Lazarus is that hell is a place of memory and remorse. The rich man didn't have the luxury of eroding into a zombie-like creature void of consciousness. He could remember his sins. I imagine that he experienced the emotional pain of regret as he remembered the many opportunities he had to show love yet chose to be selfish instead. He contemplated the likelihood that unless they were warned about this place and repented of their selfish ways, his five brothers would also plunge into the same dungeon of torment that he was experiencing, yet he was powerless to do anything about it.

The fact that the rich man craved water to quench his thirst yet was unable to obtain it shows that hell is a place of insatiable and tormenting desire. Have you ever been truly thirsty? A person who is truly thirsty is driven to satisfy that craving. Imagine how thirsty you would be in such a hot place and how horrible it would be to never again taste even a drop of water. But what about other cravings? Have you ever seen drug addicts experience the pain of withdrawal when they could not obtain drugs? The unfulfilled craving practically drives them mad. What will it be like for those who cultivated an addiction to drugs, alcohol, pornography, and other sinful pleasures when they still incessantly crave them yet are unable to fulfill their sinful desires or distract themselves with carnal comforts?

The Anguish of Hell Is Eternal

Jesus' story of the rich man and Lazarus makes it clear that hell is a world without hope of escape. After seeing Abraham in heaven and begging him to bring a drop of water for relief, the rich man is told plainly, "No one can cross over to you from here, and *no one can cross over to us from there*."

This mention of hell being a place that can never be escaped is not an isolated instance. Nearly every Bible passage that mentions hell and the punishment of the wicked also mentions the eternal nature of it. Please read the following verses and note the emphasis on the *eternal* nature of suffering in hell:

> The worms that eat them *never* die, and the fire that burns them is *never* put out. (Mark 9:48 GNT)

> . . . will punish those who do not know God and do not obey the gospel of our Lord Jesus. They will be punished with *everlasting* destruction. (2 Thessalonians 1:8–9 NIV)

There are some who teach that the torment of hell will eventually end, but this is clearly not what the Bible teaches. Jesus said of the wicked, "And these will go away into *everlasting* punishment, but the righteous into *eternal* life" (Matthew 25:46 NKJV). Just as the life that the righteous inherit is *eternal* in duration, so the punishment that the wicked suffer is *everlasting*.

In Revelation 14:10–11, God dispatched a powerful angel to give this solemn warning to those who were being tempted to worship the Antichrist, saying that those who do so "will be tormented with fire and burning sulfur in the presence of the holy angels and the Lamb. The smoke of their torment will rise *forever and ever*, and *they will have no relief day or night*." But sinful human beings aren't the only ones who will suffer in the lake of fire. Revelation 20:10 promises that "the devil, who had deceived them, was thrown into the fiery lake of burning sulfur, joining the beast and the false prophet. There they will be tormented *day and night forever and ever*." How can the eternal nature of suffering in hell be stated any more clearly?

Hell Is a Literal Place

Throughout the years, many have tried to explain away the biblical descriptions of hell by saying they are merely figurative and symbolic. However, the Bible never says that hell is not real. Over and over again, in passage after passage, it describes hell as a physical and literal place. Just as the biblical descriptions of eternity in the kingdom of heaven are literal, so are the descriptions of the torment of hell. The many descriptions of emotional and physical anguish in hell are not exaggerations; they are revealed to us as God's solemn and loving warning to motivate us to follow Jesus and avoid this place of punishment.

In Jesus' story of the rich man and Lazarus, He said that the rich man worried that his five brothers, who were still living, would not take the biblical warnings of hell seriously, and wanted to somehow send a message to convince them that hell was real so that they could avoid this place of torment. God made it clear that the Scriptures already warned about this place of eternal punishment, and if his brothers would not take the biblical warnings about hell seriously, they would not be able to be convinced any other way. I think we need to take this warning seriously and accept what the Bible tells us about hell at face value rather than trying to explain it away using our own foolish rationalizations and carnally driven arguments.

Just as the biblical descriptions of eternity in the kingdom of heaven are literal, so are the descriptions of the torment of hell.

The prophet Isaiah prophesied that hell would literally be visible in the new heavens and new earth:

> "As surely as my new heavens and earth will remain, so will you always be my people, with a name that will never disappear," says the Lord. "All humanity will come to worship me from week to week and from month to month. And as they go out, they will see the dead bodies of those who have rebelled against me. For the worms that devour them

> will never die, and the fire that burns them
> will never go out. All who pass by will view
> them with utter horror." (Isaiah 66:22–24)

In this passage, God is giving us some insight into life on earth when Jesus returns and reigns from Jerusalem. First, He promises that there will be new heavens and a new earth. Then He affirms that Israel will be His people forever. Next, He describes a regular flow of worshipers from every nation going into and coming out of the city of Jerusalem to worship Jesus. As they leave the city to begin their voyage back home, they will somehow be able to see the bodies of those who are suffering in hell. The passage explicitly refers to the inhabitants of hell as "those who have rebelled against me." Apparently, there will be some type of way for the inhabitants of the new earth, who are enjoying Jesus' leadership, to see the consequences of rebellion against Jesus and be gripped by the horror of it. Why would Jesus intentionally place this window into hell in a conspicuous place where everyone can see it? I imagine that it serves as a warning to remind people of the consequences of sin and to impart a healthy fear of the Lord into them so that they won't depart from Him.

There Are Varying Degrees of Punishment in Hell

The Bible unapologetically reveals hell as a real place of everlasting torment—a place where the torment experienced is physical, spiritual, emotional, and relational. While everyone in hell experiences torment, the Bible does indicate that there will be some variation in the degree of punishment for its inhabitants. The severity of eternal punishment will be according to the amount of truth that each person was given yet rejected. Though all the inhabitants of hell will be eternally tormented for rejecting the light they were given, those who have less revelation of God will be punished less severely than those who were given more revelation of God. For example, Romans 2:12–16 indicates that those who had access to the law of Moses and rejected it will be punished more severely than those who did not have the law of Moses. And Hebrews 10:26–31 makes clear that those who once knew Christ and then turned away from following Him will experience greater punishment than those who rejected the law of Moses.

How Does God Respond to the Horror of Hell?

The reality of hell motivated Jesus to die on the cross in our place. It is important to remember that God did not create human beings to suffer eternal punishment in hell. He created us to enjoy Him and His creation forever, but He does not force Himself upon us against our will. We must choose to love God and His wonderful ways. Hell was created as the place of punishment for those who choose to reject God and embrace a sinful nature that rebels against Him. When we choose the path of obedience, it leads to the life He created us for. However, when we choose the path of disobeying God, it always leads to death and punishment.

Does God delight in the suffering of those who choose to reject Him? Absolutely not! "Do I take any pleasure in the death of the wicked? declares the Sovereign Lord. Rather, am I not pleased when they turn from their ways and live?" (Ezekiel 18:23 NIV). This desire to make a way for guilty sinners to be cleansed from their sin and change their eternal future is what motivated Jesus to come to earth and suffer on the cross in our place.

> You see, at just the right time, when we were still powerless, Christ died for the ungodly. Very rarely will anyone die for a righteous person, though for a good person someone might possibly dare to die. But God demonstrates his own love for us in this: While we were still sinners, Christ died for us. (Romans 5:6–8 NIV)

> For God so loved the world that he gave his one and only Son, that whoever believes in him shall not perish but have eternal life. For God did not send his Son into the world to condemn the world, but to save the world through him. Whoever believes in him is not condemned, but whoever does not believe stands condemned already because they have not believed in the name of God's one and only Son. (John 3:16–18 NIV)

How Should We Respond to the Horror of Hell?

I'm proud of you for making it through this chapter. I realize that it is not pleasant to think about this subject, and it is tempting to skip over these passages of Scripture. But God purposely put these descriptions of eternal punishment in the Bible because He loves us and wants us to avoid this awful fate. God is love, and love warns.

It is healthy for us to meditate on these passages and take them to heart. Heeding the biblical warnings of hell empowers us to cling to the good news that Jesus saves, walk closely with God, and aggressively turn away from sin. One of the essential keys that helped me overcome sexual immorality in my life was meditating upon the many Bible passages that clearly say the sexually immoral will be in the lake of fire. Because I believed these warnings, I was extra motivated to resist lustful thoughts and do whatever it took to live in purity.

Additionally, knowing what the Bible says about the reality of hell should urge us to lovingly warn people about how to avoid hell through believing the gospel and submitting to Jesus as Lord. We should heed the words God spoke to the prophet Ezekiel:

> When I say to a wicked person, "You will surely die," and you do not warn them or speak out to dissuade them from their evil ways in order to save their life, that wicked person will die for their sin, and I will hold you accountable for their blood. But if you do warn the wicked person and they do not turn from their wickedness or from their evil ways, they will die for their sin; but you will have saved yourself. (Ezekiel 3:18–19 NIV)

If we truly love people, we will speak the truth to them about sin and eternal punishment, tenderly warning them to flee the wrath to come by believing and obeying the gospel of Jesus Christ.

Knowing the final end of the rebellion also gives us solid hope that justice truly will prevail on the earth. The curse will not continue forever. The earth will be restored like new again, and all God's people will flourish forever under Jesus' magnificent leadership. In the next chapter, we will explore what the Bible says about the fully restored earth.

Check It Out in the Bible for Yourself

1. Read Luke 16:19–31. What does this passage teach us about eternal punishment?

2. Read Isaiah 66:22–24; Revelation 20:10–15; 21:7–8; 14:10–11; Matthew 25:41; 25:46; Mark 9:47–48; and 2 Thessalonians 1:8–9. What do these passages teach about eternal punishment?

3. How do these truths about eternal punishment make you feel? Is there anything these Bible passages say about eternal punishment that is different from what you have always thought was true?

4. In light of what you have learned about eternal punishment in this chapter, is there anything you need to change in your life? What are you going to do to respond to what the Holy Spirit is teaching you?

5. For further study on this topic, go to my YouTube channel called *5 State Revival*. Look up the playlist titled *The End Times for Beginners* and watch:

- Video 5: "Introducing Jesus the Judge"
- Video 6: "How Can a Merciful God Also be a God of Wrath?"
- Video 7: "Six Reasons to Celebrate Jesus as a Judge"
- Video 27: "The Final Rebellion and Judgment"
- Video 28: "What Does the Bible Say About Hell?"

7

Paradise: A Sneak Peek at the New Earth

W*hat is the biggest thing on Your heart that you want people to receive from this study?* This is the question I asked the Lord in prayer as I prepared to teach an extended series through the book of Revelation to my church. His answer came swiftly into my mind, and I felt the inspiration of the Spirit as He spoke it: *I want my people to be excited about their future!*

God is a loving Father who has prepared something immensely wonderful for His children to enjoy with Him. It is the ultimate gift of living in the kingdom of heaven forever. He wants us to think about this gift and be as excited to experience it with Him as He is to experience it with us. For this reason, God encourages His people to "set your sights on the realities of heaven" and to "think about the things of heaven" (Colossians 3:1–2).

When you think about your eternal future with God, what images come into your mind? Many believers rarely think about eternity because they don't know what it looks like. Instead of an eager anticipation to experience their eternal future, they often have just a general conviction that heaven will somehow be great, and a vague, misinformed idea that they will spend eternity perpetually floating on clouds, playing harps, seeing angels fly by, and singing worship songs forever. While that sounds peaceful and certainly better than the alternative of being in hell, it also sounds boring. No wonder they are not excited about it. Thankfully, that is not what the Bible says eternal life in God's kingdom will be like.

The key to growing heartfelt enthusiasm for our eternal future is to get a clearly defined, biblically inspired picture of eternity shining brightly in our minds. How can we fix our eyes on the realities of heaven when we don't have a clear portrait of what it will actually be like? How can we think about a picture we have never seen? This is why God gives us detailed information in His Word concerning what His eternal kingdom will be like. He knows that we can't get excited about something until we have a clear vision of what it will actually be like.

For example, I love to travel the world and do fun things in new places, but I've discovered that I don't genuinely get excited about going someplace until I understand the details about what makes it so fun. I may hear that an island in the Caribbean Sea is a great place to visit, but it doesn't grip my heart with excitement until I go online to watch the videos of people snorkeling in crystal-clear water, swimming among vast schools of exotic, beautiful fish, and reveling in brightly colored coral reefs. I see the pictures of people eating delicious lobster, drinking fresh coconut juice, and lounging peacefully in a hammock hanging between two bent-over palm trees on a white sandy beach. Then I get a clear picture in my mind of how fun this place could be. I start imagining myself in the picture watching the sunset over the emerald sea while on a romantic walk with my wife. The longing in my heart to go to that island grows in proportion to the clarity of the picture in my mind. The more detail I learn about a place causes my vision of it to become clearer, and my longing to experience it becomes stronger.

We acquire excitement about our eternal future in a similar way. God has a clear and detailed eternal vision of what His finished plans for His kingdom on earth will be like, and His heart is burning with desire to see it completed. As we study and meditate on the biblical passages that describe what the new earth will be like, we can see His vision for our eternal future and imagine ourselves in the picture. When the picture of eternity that glistens in God's mind becomes clear in ours, our hearts will burn with the same passionate longing to experience it forever.

Introducing the New Earth

Perhaps the grandest picture of God's kingdom on the new earth in the entire Bible is found in Revelation 21:1–22:5. In this passage, God assures us that His master plan for people and the earth will be completed. Then He shows us a sneak peek of the finished product by giving us a brief tour of the new Jerusalem, which will be the capital city of the new earth. Let's explore this passage together to catch God's vision for our eternal future:

> Then I saw a new heaven and a new earth, for the old heaven and the old earth had disappeared. And the sea was also gone. And I saw the holy city, the new Jerusalem, coming down from God out of heaven like a bride beautifully dressed for her husband.
>
> I heard a loud shout from the throne, saying, "Look, God's home is now among his people! He will live with them, and they will be his people. God himself will be with them. He will wipe every tear from their eyes, and there will be no more death or sorrow or crying or pain. All these things are gone forever."
>
> And the one sitting on the throne said, "Look, I am making everything new!" And then he said to me, "Write this down, for what I tell you is trustworthy and true." And he also said, "It is finished! I am the Alpha and the Omega—the Beginning and the End. To all who are thirsty I will give freely from the springs of the water of life. (Revelation 21:1–6)

The passage begins with the apostle John watching the new Jerusalem descend from heaven to earth and announcing that the old heaven and old earth have been replaced by the new. Some theologians believe this means that the present earth we are living on today will be completely destroyed and replaced by a brand-new earth that God will create from scratch. I don't believe that is the meaning of this passage. As I stated in chapter 2, I believe this present earth that God made in Genesis 1–2 will last forever. God is not going to destroy it— He is completely redeeming it! When He says that the old earth has passed away, it means that the old order of things on earth during this present evil age, where everything is defiled by sin and under the curse, will be done away with. We see this spelled out just a few sentences later in verse 4 when God says, "He will wipe every tear from their eyes, and there will be no more death or sorrow or crying or pain. All these things are gone forever." Hallelujah!

One of my favorite Bible verses describing salvation is 2 Corinthians 5:17 (NIV84): "Therefore, if anyone is in Christ, he is a new creation; the old has gone, the new has come!" When I was born again, God didn't annihilate me, creating a new human being that was just like the old me and name it the new Jeff. No! I am the same person, but my old way of life marked by sin and the curse was replaced by my new way of life marked by righteousness, blessing, and life in Christ. This liberation from sin and the curse that people get to experience is also coming to the entire created order. When this salvation manifests in the rest of creation after Jesus returns, the transformation will be so dramatic that the Bible calls it the new heaven and the new earth. The old is gone and the new has come! The new earth will no longer be defiled by sin and the curse, but rather prosper under the new order of the kingdom of God, which is marked by righteousness and blessing.

The crown jewel of the new earth will be its capital city, the new Jerusalem.

The crown jewel of the new earth will be its capital city, the new Jerusalem. The beauty of this city is so exquisite that John says it is prepared as a bride adorned for her husband. A bride spares no expense and misses no detail in adorning herself for her husband on their wedding day. In the same way, God has spared no expense and has prepared every last detail of the heavenly city to be extravagantly adorned and presented to His bride as a wedding gift. This is a holy city of beauty and pleasure like none other, where Jesus and His bride will live in loving bliss forever.

The descending of the new Jerusalem to earth is the final step in God's restoration plan for humanity. The longing of God's heart has always been to live openly with His people on a perfect earth in a relationship marked by love and righteousness. Since Adam and Eve sinned in the Garden of Eden, God has been methodically working out His plan to redeem both people and the earth so that He can fulfill this desire. God describes the fulfillment of His dream in verse 3:

> Look, God's home is now among his people!
> *He will live with them*, and they will be his people. God himself will be with them.

The introduction of the new Jerusalem will mark the dawning of a new era on earth. Sin and all its devastating effects will be entirely vanquished from the human experience. As a result, human pain and anguish will cease to exist. From that point in history onward, there will be no more death or sorrow or crying or pain. The new Jerusalem is a city of joy!

I imagine John being overwhelmed by the magnitude of hope he experienced as he looked at this immaculate city and listened to these incredible promises. Some things can seem so incredible that our jaded nature wonders if they are just too good to be true. So in verse 5, God says, "Look, I am making everything new! Write this down, for what I tell you is trustworthy and true." It's as if God is going out of His way to assure us, *"Look, this is all really true. I am not exaggerating at all. These things are real. I really am making all things new! These are not just figurative pictures to make you feel good. These descriptions of heavenly bliss are literal."* God was so serious about fulfilling these promises that He commanded John to write His words down and quote Him word for word. God was officially going on record to state that these promises are fully reliable. Every single detail of these promises about life on the new earth will literally be fulfilled!

After assuring us of the certainty of these promises, God then assures the human race of His eagerness to share these wonders with us and invites us to partake of them, saying, "To all who are thirsty I will give freely from the springs of the water of life" (Revelation 21:6). If anyone is thirsty to experience the eternal life and bliss being described in this passage, God will freely give it through His Son Jesus.

The Architectural Beauty of the New Jerusalem

The new Jerusalem will be the most dazzling and desirable city of the restored earth. As the capital city of God's kingdom on the new earth, it is the ultimate blending of natural, spiritual, and architectural beauty. John was escorted by an angel to actually see it for himself and described what he saw:

> So he took me in the Spirit to a great, high mountain, and he showed me the holy city, Jerusalem, descending out of heaven from God. It shone with the glory of God and sparkled like a precious stone—like jasper as clear as crystal. (Revelation 21:10–11)

As John approached the city from a distance, he notes that his first impressions were of the size and light that shines from the city. The city is so massive that it actually appears as a vast and lofty mountain. Adding to the awe-inspiring size of the heavenly city is its radiant beauty. John records that the mountainous city is radiant with the glory of God, creating a sparkling display as the light of His glory pulsates from His throne in the heart of the city and pierces through the vast array of precious gems that adorn the city. The effect is so brilliant that "the city has no need of sun or moon, for the glory of God illuminates the city, and the Lamb is its light" (Revelation 21:23). As if that were not impressive already, the following verse goes on to say that the rest of the nations on the new earth outside of the new Jerusalem will be able to walk in its light!

Next, John records the physical dimensions of the city in verses 12–21. In particular, he describes in great detail the wall that surrounds the city. Prepare to be impressed!

> The city wall was broad and high, with twelve gates guarded by twelve angels. And the names of the twelve tribes of Israel were written on the gates. There were three gates on each side—east, north, south, and west. The wall of the city had twelve foundation stones, and on them were written the names of the twelve apostles of the Lamb. The angel who talked to me held in his hand a gold measuring stick to measure the city, its gates, and its wall. When he measured it, he found it was a square, as wide as it was long. In fact, its length and width and height were each 1,400

> miles. Then he measured the walls and found them to be 216 feet thick (according to the human standard used by the angel). The wall was made of jasper, and the city was pure gold, as clear as glass. The wall of the city was built on foundation stones inlaid with twelve precious stones: the first was jasper, the second sapphire, the third agate, the fourth emerald, the fifth onyx, the sixth carnelian, the seventh chrysolite, the eighth beryl, the ninth topaz, the tenth chrysoprase, the eleventh jacinth, the twelfth amethyst. The twelve gates were made of pearls—each gate from a single pearl! And the main street was pure gold, as clear as glass.

The new Jerusalem will be by far the largest geographic city the world has ever seen. It measures approximately 1,400 miles in both its length and width. That is nearly 2 million square miles and about half the size of the continental United States. To compare, the world's largest city in 2015 was Tokyo; it measures approximately 5,300 square miles.[27] But there's more, because the city is built on a mountain that also stretches 1,400 miles high. The highest point on earth today is the peak of Mount Everest, which stands about six miles above sea level. According to NASA, the earth's atmosphere ends at seventy-six miles above the surface of

27. https://www.worldometers.info/population/largest-cities-in-the-world/, accessed December 14, 2020.

the earth.[28] That means that the top of the new Jerusalem will extend 1,324 miles into what is currently called outer space!

The new Jerusalem is surrounded by a wall that could easily be considered the greatest architectural wonder of the world by today's standards. It measures 5,600 miles in length and is 216 feet thick, making its thickness about three-quarters the length of an American football field. It is built with jasper and pure gold, making the city walls transparent, like glass that you can see through. There are twelve gates leading into the city, three on each of its four sides. How big is a gate leading through a 216-foot-thick wall? The Bible says that each of these massive gates is made from a *single pearl*! The wall of the new Jerusalem is built upon twelve foundation stones, each one named after one of the original twelve apostles. These foundation stones are covered with twelve types of precious gems, representing a variety of beautiful colors.

The wall is only the beginning of the extravagant beauty of the new Jerusalem. John goes on to say that there is a main street in the city that is also made from pure gold as clear as glass. I can only try to picture how big the main street of a 1,400-mile-long city would be. I imagine it would be like a super highway. Can you imagine what it would be like to drive on a see-through

---

28. https://www.reference.com/science/many-miles-earth-space-e72d2cf4e-ec2da64#, accessed December 14, 2020.

highway? Only God Himself could calculate the cost of constructing a city that is this large and made with pure gold and precious gems.

The Spiritual Atmosphere of the New Jerusalem

After describing the architectural splendor of the heavenly city, John moves on to describe its spiritual atmosphere:

> I saw no temple in the city, for the Lord God Almighty and the Lamb are its temple. And the city has no need of sun or moon, for the glory of God illuminates the city, and the Lamb is its light. The nations will walk in its light, and the kings of the world will enter the city in all their glory. Its gates will never be closed at the end of day because there is no night there. And all the nations will bring their glory and honor into the city. Nothing evil will be allowed to enter, nor anyone who practices shameful idolatry and dishonesty—but only those whose names are written in the Lamb's Book of Life. (Revelation 21:22–23)

The new Jerusalem is much more than just a breathtaking architectural wonder; the entire city is a worship center. There is no temple in the city where everyone goes to worship God because every section of the city is filled with God's presence and inspires worship. Imagine living in an environment where everything around you is so lovely that it pulls your heart into adoration of Jesus. In heaven, Jesus is the delight of every person. There is no sorrow or pain—only testimonies of God's goodness and faithfulness. Each aspect of the city expresses a different facet of God's nature that fills us with pleasure to the core of our being. Everyone is happy, thankful to God, and filled with love for each other. This is God's family rejoicing in their Father's kingdom and enjoying one another's companionship.

The new Jerusalem is much more than just a breathtaking architectural wonder; the entire city is a worship center.

The new Jerusalem is also a secure and holy city. The gates of the city will never be closed because there is no fear, insecurity, or sense of danger on the new earth. It is the home of a holy God and His holy people. Only holy people will enter the heavenly city. On the new earth, there will be no evil spirits, evil people, or any type of evil influence. It is a temptation-free zone! In contrast to this present evil age where we need to constantly resist the temptations that come from living in a sinful world, everything on the new earth will actually inspire us to love, obey, worship, and fear God.

The New Jerusalem Is a Natural Wonder

In Revelation 22:1–2, John describes yet another aspect of the splendor of the New Jerusalem: it will be the ultimate natural, earthly paradise.

> Then the angel showed me a river with the water of life, clear as crystal, flowing from the throne of God and of the Lamb. It flowed down the center of the main street. On each side of the river grew a Tree of Life, bearing twelve crops of fruit, with a fresh crop each month. The leaves were used for medicine to heal the nations.

There is a majestic river in the heart of the new Jerusalem whose crystal-clear waters spring forth from God's throne and course along the center of its main street. Its water has the supernatural ability to impart life. The life-giving potential of this water is so dynamic that the trees growing alongside it, whose roots are being nourished by the water, are described as trees of life. These trees are robust and healthy, bearing a fresh crop of fruit every single month. In fact, their roots are charged with so much life from the river that the leaves are actually used to bring healing to nations after Jesus returns.

This is one of my favorite parts of life in the new Jerusalem. Can you imagine how beautiful it would be to see a crystal-clear river running down a street of pure gold with robust trees towering along its banks, highlighted with the dazzling light of glory that shines from God's throne? When I get to the new Jerusalem, I fully plan to spend lots of time in this pleasure park, swimming in the river, drinking its water, and eating the mouthwatering fruit while playing with friends and singing with angels as I worship Jesus for yet another perfect day.

The natural paradise aspect of the new earth, along with the trees of life, shows the full restoration of the Garden of Eden on earth. John continues:

> No longer will there be a curse upon anything. For the throne of God and of the Lamb will be there, and his servants will worship him. And they will see his face, and his name will be written on their foreheads. And there will be no night there—no need for lamps or sun—for the Lord God will shine on them. And they will reign forever and ever. (Revelation 22:3–5)

On the new earth, there will be no curse upon anything. This is what God has always intended for life on earth to be like! Everybody will be blessed with perfect health and supernatural energy. All vegetation will be blessed to flourish and multiply, with no weeds and no fruitless or leafless trees. God will live on the earth with His people forever. There will be magnificent cities, highways, homes, gardens, vineyards, animals, rivers, mountains, families, friendships, delicious food, and righteous governments. Righteous people in right relationship with God will populate the whole planet and govern it according to God's wisdom. Whatever we put our hand to will be blessed to prosper.

Is This Too Good to Be True?

Does this sound too good to be true? Are you hesitant to fully buy into these exciting promises in fear that you may end up disappointed? Then hear the angel's concluding words to John in Revelation 22:6 and be encouraged:

> Then the angel said to me, "Everything you have heard and seen is trustworthy and true. The Lord God, who inspires his prophets, has sent his angel to tell his servants what will happen soon."

Did you hear that? *Everything you have read in John's description of the new earth is trustworthy and true and will happen soon!* God loves us and wants His children to be genuinely gripped with overflowing confidence and enthusiasm that these things will be so. Therefore, these clear promises and vivid descriptions have been recorded in the Scriptures so that we may believe. This is why the apostle Paul wrote:

> May the God of hope fill you with all joy and peace in believing [through the experience of your faith] that by the power of the Holy Spirit you will abound in hope and overflow with confidence in His promises. (Romans 15:13 AMP)

Paradise: A Sneak Peek at the New Earth

The Bible encourages us to think about the biblical promises of heaven and to get our hopes up as we contemplate what our eternal future in God's kingdom will be like. It's exciting! My prayer for you as you read this book is that God would help you grasp His eternal vision intellectually so that the vision would grasp your heart emotionally and devotionally.

This type of hope has a profound effect on how we live during our brief years in this present age. When God's vision for eternity becomes clear in our minds and rooted in our hearts with deep conviction, it changes us for the better. The kingdom of God becomes more real and desirable to us. The glitz and seduction of the world becomes less appealing because we see it for the shallow and empty mirage that it really is.

Seeing God's eternal plan gives us true discernment to recognize the difference between the things that have eternal value and the things that don't. We begin to value the things that are most important—the things God values most—and zealously give ourselves to those noble virtues and activities. We are not as easily shaken by trials and hardships; in fact, we begin seeing them as something that is working for our eternal benefit.[29] Staying intimately connected to God's eternal vision makes us less prone to fall away from the faith, while strengthening a joyful, steadfast spirit within us. It also emboldens our witness for Jesus and fortifies our soul against vices like fear, intimidation, insecurity, covetousness, despair, and vain ambition.

---

29. See 2 Corinthians 4:16–18.

Life is short. Resolve in your heart to be a person who lives for eternity. Those who sacrificially live for God's eternal vision will never regret it. They will be the happiest people on earth both in this age and the age to come!

Check It Out in the Bible for Yourself

1. Read Revelation 21:1–22:5. Which aspects of the new Jerusalem are you the most excited to experience?

2. How is this description of eternal life on the new earth different from the way you envisioned heaven before?

3. How does this description of life on the new earth make you feel toward God? How does it make you feel about your future?

4. In light of what you learned in this passage of Scripture, how should you live?

5. For further study on this topic, go to my YouTube channel called *5 State Revival*. Look up the playlist titled *The End Times for Beginners* and watch video 29, "Paradise: God's Master Plan Is Completed," and video 30, "Paradise: Heaven on Earth."

Looking Ahead

T his is book number one in a series of short books
called *The End Times for Beginners*. This series
is designed to give you a basic understanding of
what the Bible says concerning Jesus' return, the events
that lead up to His return, and the events that follow His
return. Each book is designed to build upon the previous
book and will give you another bite-sized piece of information to add to your knowledge. By the time you finish
the series, you will have a solid understanding of the main
biblical points concerning the end times that will set you
up for a lifetime of deeper study. Here is an overview of
the books in this series:

- **Book 1:** Explains God's eternal plan to reign on earth
  with His people and gives a simple overview of the
  big-picture storyline of the whole Bible.

- **Book 2:** Explores the beauty of Jesus in His identity
  as a loving bridegroom, majestic king, and righteous
  judge. Although God has always functioned in these
  roles throughout history, these three aspects of His

nature are displayed in an especially prominent way in the end times.

- **Book 3:** Explains the significance of Israel in God's plan to bless all nations on earth and shows how the Gentile church will partner with the Holy Spirit to bring Israel into her calling so that God's eternal plans for all nations can be fulfilled. It is impossible to interpret end-times Bible passages correctly without understanding God's eternal plans for Israel.

- **Book 4:** Talks about the major events and prophetic signs that will lead up to and signal the return of Jesus, including the birth-pangs signs, the great tribulation, the rise of the antichrist empire, the abomination of desolation, the judgments mentioned in the book of Revelation, and several different movements of God that will mature and converge to usher in the final harvest of souls and bring the bride of Christ to maturity.

- **Book 5:** Focuses on the physical return of Jesus to the earth, which is the finish line where Jesus' victory over darkness is fully manifest. In this book, we will study major events that accompany Jesus' return, such as the resurrection and rapture of the saints, the battle of Armageddon, the salvation of Israel, and Jesus' triumphal entry into Jerusalem.

- **Book 6:** Explores the events that will follow the return of Jesus, including the millennial reign of Christ, the wedding supper of the Lamb, the restoration of nations and the rebuilding of cities with Jesus, the final rebellion, and the final judgment.

- **Book 7:** The final book of the series will explore the many biblical passages instructing us how to live victoriously in light of the end times and eternity. This will equip us with biblical wisdom for a fruitful and unshakable lifestyle that yields the greatest joy and eternal rewards.

About the Author

J eff Mann is a church planter, Bible teacher, disciple-maker, author, and member of the Pastoral team at James River Church in Huron, South Dakota. He graduated from Central Bible College in Springfield, Missouri with a degree in Biblical Studies. His ministry focus is to help people love Jesus passionately, live in purity, and walk in the power of the Holy Spirit as they make disciples of Jesus among the nations.

You can follow Jeff by listening to his *5-State Revival* podcast, or by visiting his 5-State Revival Facebook page and Youtube channel, where you can listen to teaching on topics such as evangelism training, church planting and missions, end-times and eternity, loving God, prayer and fasting, and living a focused life.

RELENTLESS
passion

Encounter God. Burn with
passion for Jesus.

Jeff Mann

Is Jesus your first love?

The salvation experience does not introduce us to a religion; it baptizes us into a passionate relationship with God!

Relentless Passion calls Christians to pursue passion in their relationship with God, and equips them with the tools to sustain it for a lifetime. This book will help you:

- Position yourself for life-changing encounters with God

- Practice the art of interacting with God

- Develop a devotional life that is consistent, vibrant, and fulfilling

- Identify and overcome obstacles that kill passion

- Recapture your spiritual vitality while overcoming boredom and passivity

Available for purchase on Amazon.com.

CPSIA information can be obtained
at www.ICGtesting.com
Printed in the USA
BVHW041639200521
607644BV00018B/1113